CW01083993

THROUGH THE WA
BAPTISM AND THE CHRI

The Croall Lectures, 1987
New College, Edinburgh

THROUGH THE WATERS: BAPTISM AND THE CHRISTIAN LIFE

by

DAVID S. M. HAMILTON

T & T CLARK
EDINBURGH

T & T CLARK LTD
59 GEORGE STREET
EDINBURGH EH2 2LQ
SCOTLAND

First published 1989

ISBN 0 567 09532 0 HB

British Library Cataloguing in Publication Data
Hamilton, David S. M.
Baptism and the Christian life.
1.   Christian church. Baptism
I.   Title
265'.1

ISBN 0 567 29178 2

Typeset by C. R. Barber & Partners (Highlands) Ltd
Printed and bound in Great Britain by Billing & Sons Ltd, Worcester

ACKNOWLEDGEMENTS

I am very grateful to the following for the opportunity to make quotations from copyright material:

Basic Books Inc.: *Psychoanalytic Theory, Therapy and the Self*, by Harry Guntrip; Professor Ernest Best and Cambridge University Press: *The Letter of Paul to the Romans*; The Church of Scotland Panel on Worship and Oxford University Press: *An Order for Holy Baptism*; SCM Press: *Baptism in the Holy Spirit* by James D. G. Dunn, *Christianity Rediscovered* by Vincent J. Donovan, *Jesus, the Man and the Myth*, by James P. Mackey, *Letters and Papers from Prison*, by Dietrich Bonhoeffer, and *The Shaking of the Foundations* by Paul Tillich; Faber & Faber Ltd.: "Water", from *The Whitsun Weddings* by Philip Larkin; Professor Robert W. Jenson and Fortress Press: *Visible Words*; A. J. M. Wedderburn and J. C. B. Mohr (Paul Siebeck) Tubingen for *Baptism and Ressurection*.

CONTENTS

FOREWORD

I am most grateful to the Trustees of the Croall Lectureship for the privilege of giving the lectures which are the basis of this book, within New College where students down the years have been taught to listen and respond to both the richness of the past and the complexity and possibility of the present. My thanks go to Professor James Mackey, Dean of the Faculty, Dr. Alan Lewis (now of Austin Seminary, Texas), and their colleagues for their kindness, and for finding space in a busy curriculum for the lectures to be delivered. I should like to express my particular appreciation to Professor Ernest Best for his guidance and advice, and to Mrs. Jean Gardner for unbounded patience and enthusiasm in the typing and preparing of one version after another. Special thanks go to my wife, Isabel, for all her encouragement and support, from start to finish.

The background to what follows lies in many conversations with people about what baptism stands for, and what living the life of a baptized Christian in the world calls for – with young couples with a new child to baptize; with adults of all ages, some new to the Faith, others discovering it anew and seeking, they believe, a new baptism; with people confused or ignorant; with parents deeply puzzled and hurt because the church with its careful regulations seemed to be rejecting them and their child. These are the people who have made me think about baptism, sharing something of their bafflement, searching, hurt and even resentment. What I have to say is essentially pastoral rather than dogmatic theology.

Sacraments to many, inside the church as well as outside, seem to say the wrong things – warnings instead of invitations, obligations instead of gifts, law instead of grace,

No instead of Yes. Yet they are meant to be centres of disclosure. They should expand, not narrow, our thinking. They should be 'doors to the sacred'.

To many, however, the doors seem shut, for they believe that beyond lies a no-go area, much too difficult and hazardous for the ordinary person, lay or minister. It is to people like these that what follows is addressed. Baptism needs to be thought about, talked and even argued about, throughout the church and beyond it. That is how we shall, all of us, make it our own, and grasp and hold its rich gift.

Chapter One

IMAGES

For a great many people, inside the church as well as outside, baptism is altogether mystifying. As a ceremony of naming, or of blessing by the church, or as a dramatic gesture of self-dedication, it may make some sense. But many settle for that because beyond that they cannot see a meaning in it, not even meaning in water, poured or immersed in, which is the central action which gives this sacrament its name. Reactions may range from amused puzzlement all the way to deeply felt perplexity. The puzzled and the perplexed may well include the theologically trained, as well as those whose faith is felt and intuited rather than thought out. Many of those who are responsible for teaching and guiding the people of God will privately admit that where this central event in the church's life is concerned they are themselves unclear, perhaps even unconvinced.

It is important to recognise that this state of affairs exists. Part of the problem is that ministers and lay people are often unwilling to admit to one another that they have difficulties, and that they are embarrassed at their uncertainty and lack of confidence within what they know is an important area. The nature of the problem then is not only, nor mainly, doctrinal, a question of getting the theology right. The problem lies deeper. Some theological confusion we can live with; absolute clarity is not promised, and we have no right to demand it. But, as I shall argue, the baptism problem has a deeper significance, because it concerns the very basis of Christian faith and living, and the way in which what we believe and what we are relate to one another. It concerns the way in which the life we live is seen from the angle of Christian belief, and the way in which Christian belief is seen from the standpoint of life in the world.

This difficulty can be put another way. In our thinking we rely to an important degree on images to link together different fields of our experience. Images, word-pictures, enable us to explore and understand what is complex and unfamiliar, to communicate our experience to others, to put it into words, and so to share in a common understanding. Where there are no such images, or where images are not shared and do not connect with those of others, communication, exploration, and thinking together become virtually impossible. Let me illustrate. Not long ago I was asked to lead a discussion on baptism with a group of leaders and officebearers in a local church. They had asked me to deal especially with some of the pastoral questions which arise in connection with baptism, and I explained in as straightforward a fashion as I could why in our church we baptize infants, why the regulations insist on at least one parent being a communicant member of the church, and why we consider second baptism mistaken. In the ensuing discussion they came back again and again to these issues, insistently reopening them: 'But why? ... but why not? ...' It became clear that they had their own image of baptism, and that little of what I said fitted into the frame of their image. It was not simply that they were not understanding the official church position, as if by putting it in different words the difficulties could be overcome and all become clear. We were simply not communicating: what they saw in the sacrament was largely unconnected to my dry orthodoxy. I began to see that when I said 'we believe' this or that about baptism, as if that clinched the matter, they were unimpressed and unhelped; they felt mystified and excluded. They were protesting, with scarcely concealed indignation, at the church's pontification. They must each have witnessed scores of baptism services, and each time they heard the teaching that begins the rite. Yet that teaching was saying almost nothing to them. Perhaps its sheer wordiness repelled them, so they had formed their own version of what it all meant.

Three images at least are at work. First, the popular view of baptism is very much coloured in the minds and feelings of many people by the saying of Jesus, which many associate with baptism: 'Let the children come . . .'. A picture illustrating that Gospel story is possibly the first picture of Jesus many children are shown. Baptism is seen as answering that command. When a minister takes a baby in his or her arms that minister is seen as standing in for Jesus just as the minister taking bread and wine at the table and offering it to the people is standing in for Jesus. A child brought for baptism is a child brought to Jesus. The parents are answering the Lord's invitation, so it is commonly called 'christening' and seen as a dedication and blessing. Since then it is understood as responding to the Lord's own invitation, to reject a child seems like disobeying the command to welcome the children. To refuse to baptize a child, it seems, is to take the part of the misguided disciples who rebuked those who brought their children to Jesus. This image of what baptism is I believe to be so deeply rooted in the imaginations of many church people, at all levels of sophistication, that it overrides the difficulties which church regulations about baptism try to address – the role of parents in the Christian nurture of their child, and their ability and commitment to interpret this baptism, and all that it implies, to their growing child.

Secondly, alongside that there exists for many a deep fear of the danger of dying, or even of living, unbaptized. At its most acute this can be seen in the anxiety of parents whose newborn child's life is threatened, that the baby be baptized as a matter of urgency. As social attitudes become secularised,

5

these feelings lose something of their force, but for a great many people, Christian or not, they are still there. When this is added to the belief that baptism is the church's way of extending Jesus' invitation to little children, and of helping families to respond to it, then it becomes very difficult for church members to understand baptism in any other way, or why it should apparently be available to some but not others.

A third factor in the way baptism is popularly understood is the stress in modern society upon the significance of the family. The image of the nuclear family as a close, caring unit in which parents provide generously for their children, and children grow happily and successfully, has been found by market research to be a powerful means of selling all kinds of goods and services, and its widespread and skilled use in turn reinforces that image in the minds and ambitions of young parents. The church too has come to emphasise the importance of family life, and often describes itself as a 'family of families'. Worship, Christian education and pastoral outreach are in many places structured around the family idea. Much of the thinking behind this is far from clear and confuses the model of the modern nuclear family – an essentially secular concept whose authenticity and ethic is doubtful – with the very different understanding of family relationships in the Bible. Nevertheless the family image is strong in the consciousness of church members, and it is easy to see how it contributes to a popular view of baptism. Baptism looks like the church's way of commending and celebrating family life at one of its most important moments, the arrival of a new baby, and giving the child its name and its identity with the family. To discriminate at this point between one family and another is to many unacceptable, a denial of the very way of life they think the church is there to affirm, and to embody in its own life.

Baptism then is widely seen as an important rite of passage, comparable to coming of age or marriage or a funeral, with no more reason to place conditions upon one rather than another. It does not matter that these instinctive reactions, concerning Jesus' invitation to children, fear of the consequences for a child if not baptized, and the place of the family in the life of the church, do not have any particular relation to one another. They are all immediately recognisable to everyone, they together have a cumulative force, and they constitute the strongest and clearest images of baptism held by typical church members today. 'She's been christened . . .', 'He's got his name now . . .', 'She'll thrive now . . .', relatives say. Because they express such powerful images, these are the basis of the popular 'theologies' of baptism. That they are popular is itself no bad thing. Their defect is that as we shall see they do not accord with the Biblical understandings which underly baptism, and they do not in fact provide Christians with the understanding of life for God in the world which baptism is intended to give. They proclaim no Gospel. However, because theological argument by itself will have little if any impact upon them, they will yield only to other images which can be seen and felt to be more compelling.

The Reformers borrowed a phrase from Augustine and described the sacraments as 'visible words'.[1] Augustine contrasted 'visible' with 'invisible', but the Reformers used it to compare the sacraments with the 'audible word'. They did not mean that the sacraments were illustrations of the Word, but that what was heard and seen, what was spoken and what was acted out, belong together in the proclamation and in the response to the Gospel proclaimed. Word and sacrament are through Christ bound indissolubly together.

To many people however the sacraments do not now

[1] e.g. Peter Martyr Vermigli – see *The Visible Words of God*, Joseph C. McLelland, Oliver & Boyd, 1957, pp. 129ff; and *Visible Words*, Robert W. Jenson, Fortress Press, Philadelphia, 1978.

speak. The visible word has become blurred. Mystery has become mystification. Many people seem to see only the rite, and though the words in the rite certainly refer to the Gospel verbally, the rite acted out before their eyes, however familiar, does not in itself, non-verbally, project the images in and through which they might understand more clearly and receive more powerfully the Gospel that baptism is presenting. Baptism for them has lost the power to point beyond itself to the events and the truths it is meant to declare.

It is, I believe, very important that we listen carefully to the questions that people are asking about baptism (and to the protests of those to whom, or to whose children, baptism is refused), and to sense the gut theology that lies behind them. This is important not just because there seems to be a serious breakdown in communication between teachers and people in the church, but also because this centres on the very sacrament which is intended to affirm who and what we are, what the church is, and what Christian life is founded on. If at this fundamental level meaning is not getting through, if even a sacrament has lost its power to disclose and illumine and dramatise, then we have reason to be very worried. The gap between what the theologians are saying and what the laity are seeing and hearing is alarmingly wide. Theology to many seems elitist and remote.

Thinkers and teachers who have pronounced doctrines of baptism – sometimes even 'the doctrine of baptism' – have interpreted the resistance, grumbling and indignation, the often blank incomprehension they have met with, as ignorance and spiritual shallowness. If that is indeed what is wrong, then it is the task of theologians and ministers to teach the laity what they ought to know but have forgotten, and to show them what they ought to understand but have lost grip of.

But is this not exactly where the problem lies? Theology by instruction has failed because instruction is not the way to do theology. The laity wants, and has the right to, more than the official answers to their questions; they want − and it is their right − to join in the search for the answers too. They want a theology of participation, by which they may respond in faith to the living situations from which the questions come, a theology which is the talk of the whole church. As the Reformers put the bread, the cup, and the book back into the hands of the congregation, so must we go on doing with the truth, the Word, which the sacraments enact. At Finlaystone House, near Port Glasgow, there is a very old yew tree beneath which, one day in the 1550s, John Knox celebrated the Lord's Supper with the household. It was the first Reformed communion in that part of Scotland, at a time when to celebrate it was forbidden. As so often in those exciting days everything was makeshift. For cups, Knox took from the house two big silver candlesticks, turned them upside down, and into the broad hollowed bases poured wine for the sacrament. For long afterwards they were used at communion in the parish church. The very point of sacrament is that it takes something ordinary and recognisable and adapts it so that it can contain something larger and deeper than itself, and so become a special kind of disclosure and discovery. How are we today in the *ecclesia semper reformanda* to engage people in the recovering of the sacraments − and specifically of baptism? It is for this that a theology of participation is needed − an inclusive theology that draws people in to its quest. Just as in the community of faith we are striving to develop inclusive language which speaks to and for women and men, children and adults, single and married alike, so we are called to devise a theological enterprise which includes and does not exclude, a listening rather than a predominantly addressing and didactic theology.

We need to discover the household words, pictures and images, the commonplace things, which are the very stuff of sacrament.

Theology begins where we are, and we cannot disentangle it from where we are without damage. Although we can learn from the past, and from the way in which Christians in other situations tackled their problems, never before have quite the same questions arisen in quite the same way as they now do for us. We are the experts in our own time and its problems and we must take them seriously.

This is a task for practical theology, for a coming and going between sacramental theology as it has been understood in other times and places, and the questions and discoveries of our time and place. No generation, certainly since the Reformation, has felt this task as keenly as ours. This is why the questions which people are asking must be listened to with patience and without defensiveness. And where there is not even the wherewithal to frame a question, so alienated are they from church-speak, then we must listen with greater attentiveness than ever.

C. S. Song, writing about theology in an Asian setting says:

> ... we do not have to do theology: theology is already in the making. *Theo*-logy is there because God is there. It is the *theo*-logy that precedes our theo-*logy*. Theo-*logy* without *theo*-logy is a semantic that touches neither the heart of God nor the hearts of our fellow human beings. Theology is born when we meet persons in their life and history.[2]

---

[2]C. S. Song, *Tell Us our Names: Story Theology from an Asian Perspective*, Orbis Books, New York, 1984, p. 32.

It is what another Asian theologian, Takenaka Masao of Japan, calls 'Aha-theology' – in the midst of thinking and exploring, suddenly understanding breaking through, and we say 'Aha! now I see . . .'[3] In what ways then does baptism enlighten the Christian life of the individual and of the community of faith, local or global? If sacraments are meant to be ways of seeing, of bringing home the Gospel, how can baptism help us to see meaning in our lives and in the life of the world in our time? That is where the questions are asked; that is where the people of God are, to speak or to fall silent, to protest or to condone, to be different or to compromise, to love or to shun, to stand or to fall, to live or to die. What theology is born when we meet one another in our life and history?

In his book *Christianity and Symbolism* F. W. Dillistone writes:

> . . . to find a way of allowing baptism to exercise its power within the Christian community at the deepest level of the human psyche is one of the most urgent tasks of our day.[4]

How do we go about this? One way is to consider some of the salient images which underly baptism, and try to discern those which seem most vivid and eloquent, and so most likely to enable people to receive this sacrament as a means of grace for Christian living. It is surely significant that in none of the popular images of baptism outlined above is there any reference at all to water. It is as if the sacrament has become totally detached from its element. Not all baptismal images of course are to do with water – 'adoption' or 'grafting' for

[3]See Christine Lienemann-Perrin, *Training for a Relevant Ministry*, World Council of Churches, 1981, p. 166; Takenaka Masao, "First Fruits of the New Humanity", in *Living Theology in Asia*, ed. John C. England, SCM, 1981, pp. 37–43.
[4]F. W. Dillistone, *Christianity and Symbolism*, Collins, 1955, p. 187.

instance are not − but it begins to look as if once baptism ceases to be about water and the significance of water, it also ceases to mean anything very much at all.

The root of the word 'baptism' of course means 'dipping', 'washing', or 'immersing' something in water. We shall later consider how baptism came to take on a special meaning of its own, but the starting point from which to explore its meaning is the imagery of water. It is all the more curious then to find that not only popular imagination but even some church liturgies have detached baptism from its root associations. The preamble in the Order for Baptism in the Church of Scotland *Book of Common Order 1979*, in a string of some eleven baptismal images, only once refers to water (in this case washing). This is very odd, and no doubt helps to account for the confusion in the minds of many about baptism. Philip Larkin has an intriguing poem which he calls 'Water':

> If I were called in
> To construct a religion
> I should make use of water.
>
> Going to church
> Would entail a fording
> To dry, different clothes;
>
> My litany would employ
> Images of sousing,
> A furious devout drench.
>
> And I should raise in the east
> A glass of water
> Where any-angled light
> Would congregate endlessly.[5]

[5]Philip Larkin, *The Whitsun Weddings*, London, 1964.

That reminds us vividly of the imagery that lies at the heart of our belief and our practice. Such images are not of course exclusive to Christianity. They lie deep within the collective human imagination, and it is important that it is so, for an image that is private to a particular group of people cannot be (and is not meant to be) communicated to those outside the group. It is an important aspect of the Lord's Supper and of baptism that they each begin from something universally recognisable – the sharing of food and drink, and the experience of being plunged in water. Wherever the subtle directions of baptism lead us, we must never lose touch with that fundamental, 'felt' starting point – the experience, pleasant or alarming, of water flowing over us. But it may be that as the water used for infant baptism has become less and less visible – sometimes scarcely more than a discreet dampness of the minister's fingertips – so Christians have become more and more confused about what it is meant to represent. It may be that without water unmistakeably there to focus on, people have been either driven back into a popular mythology of infancy (naming, christening, ensuring the child is in a state of grace), or else as adults driven down to a seashore or a river bank, to undergo what at least looks and feels like baptism, alongside which the genteel ceremony around the font which had been their infant baptism seems unreal and meaningless.

It is not suggested that the meaning of baptism will at once become clear if only we will use more water, as if sacramental validity could be measured in millilitres. Water there must however unmistakeably be, at the centre of what is taking place. And what is said about the water, about the one being baptized, and about all who are gathered round, must project vivid images, which can make the sacrament a telling, evocative expression of the Gospel.

The word 'image' is probably better for our purpose than 'symbol' or 'sign', for two reasons: first, because 'symbol' and 'sign' carry with them a great deal of philosophical and theological luggage which makes them apt to confuse rather than clarify; and second, because using 'image' borrows an everyday idea to help us in the far from everyday puzzles of sacramental theology. By 'image' I mean a representation, a cue, usually visual, which points beyond itself to a concept, or a person, or an event, in such a way that the image brings it vividly to our minds and helps us to understand it, explore it, and indeed recall it whenever the image is presented. A lot of money can be made out of 'imageing' – discovering images which trigger responses in us, and make us value, or want, or choose, or believe, or simply recognise, that to which the image points. This universal characteristic of human behaviour helps to sell beer, cars, politicians, and even more complex ideas like investing money or managing intimate relationships with others.

Of course it is not water in itself that is the image. Philip Larkin has to go on from saying that at the heart of a religion lies 'water' to spelling out in more detail what significance it would have. To say that baptism involves the use of water would tell us nothing of any great importance about baptism. The significance of water is complex, and leads to a cluster of images, some of which are pleasant, others disturbing, some commonplace, others mysterious. I have already suggested that some ancient baptismal images – adoption,[6] and grafting a shoot to a stock for instance – should be given secondary importance at best. Since by definition baptism involves water, water imagery has to be primary. There are in fact

---

[6]'Adoption' is a misleading term nowadays for baptism. Its Biblical usage can scarcely take account of the complex relationships between an adopted child and the adoptive parents on the one hand and the biological mother on the other. And there is not time in the liturgy to explain Romans 8 or Galatians 4.

three such primary images to be found in the Bible and the Christian tradition – cleansing or washing, deliverance from danger or death, and birth. It is not to be thought that these together say all that can be said about baptism, nor that they provide us with all we need to know about belonging and celebrating as those who are 'in Christ'. Nor, for that matter, are all three on the same plane of importance for exploring the rich seams of meaning that lie within the sacrament of baptism, and its relation to the Christian life. But I believe that we need to return again and again to these three images beyond all others in our listening to and talking with people about baptism.

There is something very odd about a sacrament which does not make sense. Here is something given to the church to be a way into the epicentre of mystery and truth, for the opening of blind eyes, so that the unreachable may be brought close, and the baffling recast in simplicity. What has happened to make baptism so intellectualised and so inaccessible? The truth is that the sacrament cannot be separated from its element, and its element cannot be separated from the images of which it speaks. Baptism cannot be understood except in terms of water, and the powerful vivid imagery which water evokes. The images come with the sacrament. They are not just the packaging: they are part of the package itself.

Chapter Two

WASHING

The Book of Acts, recounting how people responded to the proclamation of the Gospel of the crucified and risen Jesus, says:

> Now when they heard this they were cut to the heart, and said to Peter and the rest of the apostles, 'Brethren, what shall we do?' And Peter said to them, 'Repent, and be baptized every one of you in the name of Jesus Christ for the forgiveness of your sins; and you shall receive the gift of the Holy Spirit. For the promise is to you and to your children and to all that are far off, every one whom the Lord our God calls to him'. And he testified with many other words and exhorted them, saying, 'Save yourselves from this crooked generation'. So those who received his words were baptized, and there were added that day about three thousand souls. (Acts 2: 37–41.)

These verses and the pictures they project are so familiar to us that they probably do not strike us as particularly surprising. Yet is it not extraordinary that to the question people asked there apparently was an answer ready, in the form of an invitation and a rite? 'Those who received (Peter's) words were baptized'. Where did this 'baptism' come from? How did the apostles know what to do? Why did they say what they did about it? There is no institution of baptism by Jesus like that of the Supper. No warrant, no teaching, no 'This do', has come down to us. Yet the implication given by the recorder is that the apostles were ready for this moment, and knew what to do when it came. The preaching of the Gospel included the call to repentance, baptism, and the gift of the Spirit.

Matthew 28: 18–20 is often described in baptismal liturgies as 'the command of the risen Lord'.[1] It is most unlikely – most New Testament scholars would say impossible – that these words, in this Trinitarian form, are the very words of Jesus.[2] This saying is important, but for understanding the development rather than the institution of baptism: there is reason to believe that the saying existed earlier in a shortened form that omitted the words 'baptizing them'.[3] It is therefore unwise, even dishonest, to cite them blandly as if they were beyond doubt the dominical warrant for baptism, as if the difficulties do not matter, or as if liturgical usage is exempt from tiresome 'academic' questions of this kind. As with so much else in the life of the early church the likelihood is that, allowing for broad agreement, each local Christian community practised, and even understood, baptism in relation to its own special tradition. Yet there can be no doubt that there existed a basic core of tradition and of practice which made baptism one of the major uniting and consolidating forces in the church's life. W. F. Flemington has pointed out that the New Testament actually contains more references to baptism than to the Lord's Supper. This, he argues, shows that baptism had a clear and well understood meaning, so much so that far from being a matter of dispute it was appealed to to settle disputes about other matters.

[1]See for instance the Church of Scotland's *The Book of Common Order 1979*, and *An Order for Holy Baptism* (1986); the United Reformed Church's *A Book of Services*; the Church of England's *The Alternative Service Book*; and the Faith and Order Paper No. 111, *Baptism, Eucharist and Ministry*, World Council of Churches, 1982, pp. 2–17.

[2]Eduard Schweizer, *The Good News according to Matthew*, SPCK, 1976, pp. 530ff.; W. F. Flemington, *The New Testament Doctrine of Baptism*, SPCK, 1964, pp. 105ff.

[3]See e.g. A. W. Argyle, *The Gospel According to Matthew*, Cambridge University Press, 1963, p. 221f.; H. Benedict Green, *The Gospel According to Matthew*, Oxford University Press, 1975, p. 231f.

'Baptism was so significant and so universally understood as embodying the heart of the Gospel that a New Testament writer could solve a practical problem of Christian living by simply asking Christians to remember what their baptism involved'.[4] But we are still faced with the question: how did baptism arise in the church, and what did it mean? Something must already have been there, but what was it?

Although there are no words or actions of institution and command for baptism as there are for the Supper, what have come down to us, as vividly as the accounts describing the Supper, are the records of the baptism of John, and of Jesus' baptism by John. (Matthew 3: 1–17; Mark 1: 1–11; Luke 3: 1–22; John 1: 19–34). John's mission, and its baptismal sign, is highlighted in the Gospels not for its own sake but because it was to John and his baptism that Jesus came, to make this the sign of the inauguration of his mission. Jesus could however have chosen all kinds of starting-points. What then was it about John's preaching, and the baptism to which it pointed, that drew Jesus to identify himself with it, and eventually to make of it the image of his birth, life, death, and resurrection? What indeed did baptism mean to John, and what did it mean to those who listened to his urgent message, and were led by him down into the waters of the Jordan river, and there baptized?

The significance of washing as a ritual was of course not new. Washing played an important part in the obligations of the Jewish law. There were detailed rites and practices for the whole range of life, cultic, social, domestic, and personal, to guard against uncleanness and to ensure purity. (Exodus 30: 17–21, 40: 7–13; Leviticus 11–16; Numbers 19). The impurities for which such elaborate washing and sprinkling was laid

[4]"An approach to the theology of baptism", *Expository Times*, vol. 62, 1951, pp. 356–359.

down were not moral. They were contaminations which, it was taught, resulted from ordinary, often unavoidable, circumstances – contact with a dead body; eating or even touching the carcase of an animal used for food; being subject to certain skin conditions; menstruation or childbirth. Closely associated with these were washings for someone who had touched what was holy and consecrated – a priest after performing a sacrifice, or the high priest after emerging from (as well as before entering) the Holy of Holies on the Day of Atonement, or even soldiers returning home after a 'holy war'.

> This impurity (writes Roland de Vaux) is not to be understood as a physical or moral defilement, and this kind of holiness is not to be understood as a moral virtue: they are rather 'states' or 'conditions' from which men must emerge to re-enter normal life.[5]

'Normal life' meant life within the chosen and consecrated people of God, life clearly distinct from that of the pagan world. To be God's people meant to be different, and bathings and washings in the correct way at the proper time provided a means of physically demonstrating and affirming that. Particularly during and following the shocking and unnerving experience of exile, practices such as these became more carefully elaborate, and from being primarily a priestly duty were extended into the daily life of ordinary people. (Mark 7: 1–8; Luke 11: 37–41; Matthew 15: 1–9; Hebrews 9: 6–10, 10: 19–25).[6]

These washings were for purification, not for repentance

[5] *Ancient Israel: its Life and Institutions*, Darton, Longman & Todd, 1961, p. 460f.
[6] See Carl H. Kraeling, *John the Baptist*, Charles Scribner's Sons, 1951, pp. 111ff.

19

and forgiveness, and the distinction is important. That is not to say that they were mere outward rituals having no bearing on mind or heart. Jewish thought did not distinguish between body and soul, the outward and the inward, and a man who solemnly washed or bathed in accordance with the Law would believe his whole being would be purified. Yet it was tempting to believe that to fulfil the Law and to carry out the actions of purification to the letter was all that was required. Other voices, however, prophetic voices, challenged the assumption that to be ritually clean was to be a holy people, genuinely obedient to the Lord and his Law. In contrast to the complexity of the Levitical prescriptions the prophets spoke with a stark directness:

> Wash yourselves; make yourselves clean;
> remove the evil of your doings from before my eyes;
> cease to do evil, learn to do good;
> seek justice, correct oppression;
> defend the fatherless, plead for the widow.
> 'Come now, let us reason together, says the Lord:
> though your sins are like scarlet, they shall be as white as snow;
> though they are red like crimson, they shall become like wool.
> If you are willing and obedient, you shall eat the good of the land;
> but if you refuse and rebel, you shall be devoured by the sword;
> for the mouth of the Lord has spoken'. (Isaiah 1: 16–20)

> I will take you from the nations, and gather you from all the countries, and bring you into your own land. I will sprinkle clean water upon you, and you shall be clean from all your uncleannesses, and from all your idols I will cleanse you. A new heart I will give you, and a new spirit I will put within you; and I will take out of your flesh the heart of stone and

give you a heart of flesh. And I will put my spirit within you, and cause you to walk in my statutes and be careful to observe my ordinances. You shall dwell in the land which I gave to your fathers; and you shall be my people, and I will be your God. (Ezekiel 36: 24–28)

In the Psalms, this becomes a cry for forgiveness and a right relationship with God:

Have mercy on me, O God,
according to thy steadfast love;
according to thy abundant mercy
blot out my transgressions.
Wash me thoroughly from my iniquity,
and cleanse me from my sin'.

Behold, thou desirest truth in the inward being;
therefore teach me wisdom in my secret heart.
Purge me with hyssop, and I shall be clean;
wash me, and I shall be whiter than snow . . .
> (Psalm 51. See also Psalms 26, 73, etc.)

A number of different Greek words are used in the Septuagint to mean 'wash'. Among them is the word *baptizein*, the intensive or strengthened form of *baptein*. In classical Greek *baptein* meant simply 'to dip' or 'to sink'. *Baptizein* meant 'to plunge' or 'to immerse', and in the passive 'to be overwhelmed', 'to go under', or even 'to drown'. It is not used often, however, in the LXX and never with any special significance. It appears for instance in Elisha's command to Naaman to wash seven times in Jordan (II Kings 5: 10–14), and in an interesting metaphorical sense in Isaiah 21: 4, meaning 'to be overwhelmed'.

By New Testament times there were two particular practices which can be described as in a stricter sense 'baptismal'. Both have been claimed by various scholars as prototypes of John's baptism, and we must briefly consider each of them. One was Jewish proselyte baptism, the other the purificatory washings of Jewish sects such as the Essenes or the community of Qumran.

When Gentiles were converted and became Jews, their initiation into the covenant community included (for women as well as men) what was called a 'baptism', a bath, symbolising the washing away of all taint of former life, past practices and allegiances, so that, cleansed and purified, the new convert could proceed to make a sacrifice to God and fulfil the requirements of the Law. Although it looks as if proselyte baptism has had a major influence on John's baptism and on the subsequent development of Christian baptism, there are difficulties in the way of making too simple a connection. For one thing, the evidence that proselyte baptism was in use by the beginning of the first century AD is far from conclusive. Most of what is known about it comes from later Rabbinic writing, and dating its origin can only be an educated guess. There is however circumstantial evidence that it was in use by the time of John. There are certainly similarities between the two rites, but there are important differences too. In proselyte baptism, for instance, the convert washed himself in the presence of witnesses, and that contrasts sharply with John's practice. (Matthew 3: 6, 11; Mark 1: 4–5; Luke 3: 7). He performed the baptism of those who came to him, among them religious leaders who may well have presided over a proselyte baptism. Indeed the form John's baptism took was distinctive enough for him to become known as 'the Baptizer'. (This feature of John's rite is specially important in relation to the baptism of Jesus. Despite the difficulties, at the time or later, despite John's apparent reluctance and the awkwardness of the event for the church, Jesus was baptized by John – Matthew 3: 13–15; Mark 1: 9; Luke 3: 21).

The second important difference between John's baptism and the baptism of proselytes is of course the fact that, by definition, proselyte baptism was not for those who were Jews by birth. John's call was specifically addressed to Jews, though there is nothing to suggest that Gentiles were excluded. The prophetic and apocalyptic references in his preaching would however mean little to non-Jews. (Matthew 3: 7ff; Mark 1: 4–5; Luke 3: 7–9). Yet this strengthens the possibility that it was proselyte baptism which suggested to John the rite he devised. His message was that all had sinned, but most of all the covenant people themselves. They had made themselves no better than Gentiles: ". . . do not presume to say to yourselves, 'We have Abraham as our father'; for I tell you, God is able from these stones to raise up children to Abraham" (Matthew 3: 9). Those who would truly serve God had to repent and become his people all over again, in order to prepare for the one who was to come.[7]

There are grounds then for seeing a link between Jewish proselyte baptism, through John's adaptation of it, and Christian baptism. A similar link with the purifying washings of contemporary Jewish sects is less clear. There is reason to think that there were connections between, for instance, the Qumran community or the Essenes and John and his circle, and in turn with Jesus and his disciples.[8] Yet the formal and repeated ritual washings that were apparently such an

[7]For detailed discussions of this see W. F. Flemington, *The New Testament Doctrine of Baptism*, chapter 1; Karen Pusey, "Jewish Proselyte Baptism", *Expository Times*, vol. 95, 5 Feb. 1984, pp. 141–145; Oscar Cullmann, *Baptism in the New Testament*, SCM, 1950, pp. 62ff.

[8]Charles H. H. Scobie, *John the Baptist*, SCM, 1964, especially chapter VI, argues persuasively against the link with proselyte baptism and in favour of the lustrations of the Qumran community as the most likely background to John's baptism. G. R. Beasley-Murray, *Baptism in the New Testament*, Macmillan, 1962, p. 39f. sees hints of Qumran teaching in John's preaching.

important feature of life in the monastery above the Dead
Sea seem a long way from John and the Jordan baptisms.
What they had in common was a stress on purification, but
there are too many differences between the two rites to allow
a close connection. Gunther Bornkamm, writing of the
background to John's baptism, dismisses arguments for the
link with proselyte baptism, and goes on:

> ... Much more convincing is the reference to the various
> rites of baptism which we know from isolated Jewish sects in
> Palestine and Syria in the first few centuries. The Essenes also
> belong to these. But all these 'baptisms', through which the
> baptized became a member of such a community, are at best
> initial baptisms, aiming at a continued repetition of ritual
> cleansings, and not happening once for all as with John.[9]

It is necessary to give this summary of the Jewish
background to baptism in the New Testament, however
brief, not out of academic interest, but for other reasons of
practical importance. If Jewish proselyte baptism, and perhaps
also the purificatory lustrations of a Jewish sect, are models
which John and the apostles were to use, then the dominant
image in baptism as the first Christians saw it, was washing,
cleansing, purifying. Even though other more important
images were to come to express the meaning of baptism in
fresh ways, the original image of washing has stuck, and has
perplexed people to this day.

Perhaps the truth is that although John would certainly
have other contemporary 'baptisms' in mind he did not set
out to copy any one of these. John stood between what was
familiar and what was new, pointing both to the past and to
the future. 'Baptism' was something everyone who came to

[9]Gunther Bornkamm, *Jesus of Nazareth*, Hodder & Stoughton, 1960,
p. 47.

him would recognise and understand, as a symbolic washing away of what was impure. No doubt in this it owed something to both proselyte and ritual washings. But it was sufficiently different and new to distinguish it from these, and to enable it to carry an urgent message for Jews and Gentiles alike. The message of 'one crying in the wilderness' had been uttered many times before. This time the symbolism was quite new and the sense of urgency compelling. It was a call to confess sin, to repent and, as a sign of confession and repentance, to undergo baptism – not however out of individual piety, but because the Promised One was at hand, the kingdom near, the long expected retribution of God almost upon them.

John's baptism and preaching pointed forward, and it is quite conceivable that for that reason baptism might have ended there so far as Christians are concerned, for the sign of preparing for one coming was no longer relevant once the coming one had arrived. John's baptism is therefore not in itself the prototype for Christian baptism, nor in itself the reason for the rite that took place at Pentecost as if it were the most obvious thing to do. What drew John into the Gospel narratives, and made his baptism important for the church, and linked it to Pentecost, was that Jesus came to John to be baptized. This is the event, recounted and placed with deliberate care, that is the threshold to the mission of Jesus. In Mark it appears in the very first verses; in Matthew and Luke it immediately follows the prologue. The ministry of Jesus, the evangelists tell us, began with his baptism.[10] That in itself was striking enough, but there is also talk of the Spirit descending, and of a heavenly voice. (Matthew 3: 16–17; Mark 1: 10–11; Luke 3: 21–22; John 1: 32–34). These allusions point both back and forward. They echo Old

[10]See Acts 1: 22, 10: 37.

Testament words and images of the Servant Messiah, of one who when he came would be anointed with the Spirit and water, who would be King, Son and servant of the Lord. (Psalm 2: 7; Isaiah 42: 1). The events of the baptism also point forward, however, to the path of service and of filial obedience that now lies ahead. The baptism, the voice, and the descending Spirit at one and the same time declare who Jesus is, and reveal what he has come to do.[11]

The baptism of Jesus does of course pose problems. Why, people ask, did Jesus, the sinless one, submit to this? From an early stage, it seems, this perplexed the church, and created tension between the disciples of Jesus and the followers of John. There is no reference to these problems in the earliest account of Jesus' baptism. Only later, in the material special to Matthew is the difficulty stated and answered:

> Then Jesus came from Galilee to the Jordan to John, to be baptized by him. John would have prevented him, saying, 'I need to be baptized by you, and do you come to me?' But Jesus answered him, 'Let it be so now; for thus it is fitting for us to fulfil all righteousness'. Then he consented. (Matthew 3: 13–15)[12]

[11]James D. G. Dunn, *Baptism in the Holy Spirit*, SCM, 1970, analyses the interrelationships of each of the elements in the baptism: "The baptism is not part of the eschaton or of its inbreaking. It is still the baptism of John, still the preparatory rite whose fulfilment lies not in itself but awaits the future. That the fulfilment follows the performance of the rite in the case of Jesus is due not to the rite but to the person involved in it . . . It was not the rite which made the difference, since many others were baptized by John and heard and saw nothing; it was the person who made the difference. And not merely the person, for he had been living about thirty years, but the attitude with which he came. The rite played a role, and an important role at that, but not the decisive role which most sacramentalists like to give it. It was the occasion of Jesus' commitment and the means by which he expressed his submission to his Father's will. But it was only that. It was not the baptism at which the Father expressed his pleasure: it was his Son with whom he was well pleased, because he had shown his willingness for his divine mission". p. 36.

[12]See Scobie, op. cit. pp. 15f., 142–145, 147f.; and E. Hennecke, *New*

Even as late as the writing of the Fourth Gospel this was evidently a sensitive issue. The matter of fact statement in John 3: 22 that early in his ministry Jesus himself baptized is made even more puzzling by the equally matter of fact correction of this some verses later, in 4:2. This passage, 3: 22–4: 3, may be not so much about baptism as about the relation between Jesus and John, for the benefit of the church who had to deal with questions from a group still loyal to John the Baptist and his movement. What the Fourth Gospel seems to suggest at any rate helps to bridge the gap between John's baptism and Pentecost. Flemington writes, 'If . . . baptism were practised with the approval of Jesus, it becomes easier to explain why, immediately after Pentecost, baptism took its place as the normal rite of entry into the Christian community'. But C. K. Barrett, quoting this remark, comments, 'It should however be added that baptism practised during the ministry (even if historical) cannot be regarded as a sufficient explanation of the later rite'.[13]

It is usual to explain Jesus' baptism at the hands of John as an 'identification' with sinful humanity. According to this view, Jesus did not really belong with the sinners who came to hear John. Jesus' baptism, it is alleged, was not at all like that of the others – outwardly the same, perhaps, but in reality quite different, as the dove and the voice show. But if Jesus' baptism was quite different, then in what respect was it an identification with sinful men and women? So much can be made of the contrast between Jesus and the rest that it becomes very difficult to make sense of the baptism at all: instead of being one with humanity, Jesus is distanced,

Testament Apocrypha, ET ed., R. McL. Wilson, SCM, 1963, vol. I, pp. 153ff.
[13]Flemington, The New Testament Doctrine of Baptism, p.31; C. K. Barrett, The Gospel According to John, SPCK, 1955, p. 192.

divinised, and wrenched from his earthliness. Christians can become so anxious not to compromise Jesus that they overstate his otherness. This amounts to a modern version of the old heresy of Docetism, which so stressed the divinity of Christ that his incarnation was diminished and the sense in which he was 'made man for us men and for our salvation' became blurred and unreal. In modern times this heresy persists in the insistence that Jesus came only to give and never to receive, so self-sufficient that he had no need of anything people could give him. The marvel of grace is not only that it is God's giving to us, but that it is also the opportunity for us to give to God. It is from Jesus that we have seen and learned that this is what grace, and the gracious relationship, is like, and the first sign of it is in the submissiveness of his baptism. Might it have been the fact that John was the Baptizer — and not just the eschatalogical message — that drew Jesus to go out to John and ask to be baptized?

In what sense then did Jesus in his baptism identify himself with the others? Is it not possible that he too needed something in his own terms of what John's baptism held out? 'Sinlessness', though often said of Jesus, can be such a negative concept that it is unable to say anything positive about him, describing merely what he was not, rather than what he was. If sin is the barrier between humankind and God, that which distances and alienates us from God, then Jesus was different not so much because he never did anything wrong as because there were no barriers between him and God. It is this that the Fourth Gospel meditates on and marvels at: "Anyone who has seen me has seen the Father. Then how can you say 'Show us the Father'? Do you not believe that I am in the Father, and the Father is in me? . . ." (John 14: 10). Here then was the one person in whom there was complete openness to the Father, in whom repentance, *metanoia*, was a unique reality, for he was completely turned towards God. Here was the one being in whom the Spirit could wholly dwell, for whom and to whom the heavenly voice could unmistakably speak.

What is more, Jesus too was about to change his ways, to turn from his past, let it go, and take a new direction, not because there was anything wrong in his past but because this was what, for him, obedience meant. For him the conflict with sin was much more profound than anything John or his followers knew, the choices infinitely more difficult and far-reaching, as the lonely testing which significantly follows the baptism tells. That, and much more, lay ahead; the future was dark and uncertain. For now, Jesus came to be baptized with all the others, affirming his openness and readiness to do the Father's will, and the voice and the dove answered. It was not that the voice and the dove somehow made respectable what Jesus did in being baptized by John. If by some chance the narrative had made no mention of these mystical (and probably private) experiences, the significance of the baptism itself would be no different, no less profound. Jesus gave the event significance and authenticated himself by asking to be baptized by John. We must beware of any glib interpretation of what happened. Jesus is Son of God not in spite of, but because of, the strange scandal of baptism and crucifixion. This is a fundamentally important point, which underlies all we say about baptism. It is put with great clarity by James Mackey:

> If the historian does his job well enough, he will not come upon two events, or even a double event, one event or part of the event scandalous, but the other of such a divinely revelational character that it reverses the implications of the first and successfully removes its scandal (for then our conclusion would have to read: yes, Jesus was Son of God *in spite of* the fact that John the Baptizer baptized him, that is to

say, in spite of what history left to itself could tell us). No, the historian will find just one event, Jesus' baptism by John the Baptizer, and he already knows what that baptism was, and he will then be told in the same context, by use of the old enthronement theme and by reference to the coming of the Spirit of God, that the one who is here baptized is Son of God.

There is no 'in spite of' in evidence here. We are told quite plainly that this one who cleanses and purifies himself in preparation for the coming of God's reign is God's Son and bearer *par excellence* of the Spirit of God, just as later on in the resurrection kerygma we are told that this one who was judged a threat to the secure power of both ecclesiastical and civic leaders and was condemned and executed on such a charge, is God's Son and breather of God's Spirit. Apparently, in both cases, because of, not in spite of, what happened. We may prefer a different kind of Son of God. We normally do. We may be secretly quite disappointed with the one we got. We usually are. Well, that's just too bad.[14]

If the baptism of Jesus is to be more than an act of symbolic identification, a gesture, but not for real, then there has to be reality in it for Jesus himself, as John V. Taylor writes in *The Go-Between God*:

> For (Jesus) the descent of the dove was a moment of seeing and hearing, in which he realised in a deeper, clearer recognition his own role both as Son of God and as Suffering Servant, and the identity of these two Old Testament images.[15]

It is such an account as this of Jesus' baptism that then points on to the significance of the important words he has to say

[14]*Jesus, the Man and the Myth*, SCM, 1979, p. 271f.
[15]John V. Taylor, *The Go-Between God*, SCM, 1972, p. 20.

later to the disciples about baptism and suffering which we shall examine in the next chapter.

As the story unfolds, John's baptism becomes overlaid by the baptism of Jesus at his hands, an act of commitment of Father to Son and of Son to Father, the beginning of the ministry of him who was to be suffering servant, the descent of the Spirit, the heralding of the new age. With what else then would the apostles celebrate the beginning of the new community and respond to the gift of the Spirit poured out now on all flesh? With what else would they mark the repentance and surrender of those touched to the heart by what they heard, and answer their question 'What must we do'? It was very clear: they must begin where Jesus began, with baptism – baptism by water and the Spirit, in the name of Jesus. And if proselyte baptism, or the rituals of contemporary sects well known to some of them, or above all the vivid recollection of John's dramatic baptizing and their own contacts with John, each to some degree influenced the followers of Jesus, then it is the image of washing that would be reinforced for their understanding of what baptism signified.

Not only in Acts but elsewhere too in the New Testament this washing image reappears. 'You were washed, you were sanctified, you were justified in the name of the Lord Jesus Christ and the Spirit of our God' is no doubt a reference to baptism, although another less special term is used for 'washed' (I Corinthians 6: 11).[16] Yet there are hints of the dangers of too close an association of Christian with Jewish thinking and practice, signs that some Christians had not fully grasped the difference – 'Therefore let us leave the elementary doctrines of Christ and go on to maturity, not laying again a foundation of repentance from dead works

[16]*apolouo* and not *baptizein* is the word used. See F. F. Bruce, *I and II Corinthians*, Marshall, Morgan and Scott, 1971, p. 61f.

and of faith towards God, with instructions about ablutions (*baptismon*), the laying on of hands, the resurrection of the dead, and eternal judgement' (Hebrews 6: 1–6). It is not the rite but the Lord who stands behind the rite who purifies, forgives and accepts. Our trust is in him, and not in anxious repetitive searching for the assurance of forgiveness.

The stress upon baptismal cleansing which, we have suggested, was the primary image in the primitive church, remained even when other images began to enrich baptism theology. As a result, widely diverging views developed as to the right age for baptism. At one extreme were those who held that if baptism washed away all sin, then it was necessary at all costs to avoid the risk of post-baptismal sin. Instead of baptizing children, baptism should be delayed until mature adulthood, when the recklessness of youth was safely passed. The illogicality of this seems to have escaped its proponents. Tertullian for example wrote:

It follows that deferment of baptism is more profitable, in accordance with each person's character and attitude, and even age: and especially so as regards children ... It is true our Lord says, forbid them not to come to me. So let them come when they are growing up, when they are learning, when they are taught what they are coming to: let them be made Christians when they have become competent to know Christ ... Let them first learn how to ask for salvation, so that you may be seen to have given to one that asketh. With no less reason might the unmarried also be delayed until they either marry or are firmly established in continence: until then, temptation lies in wait for them, for virgins because they are ripe for it, and for widows because of their wandering about. All who understand what a burden baptism is will have more fear of obtaining it than of its postponement.[17]

[17]*On Baptism*, 18 (PL 1, 1329), ET ed. Ernest Evans, SPCK, 1964,

Among those baptized as adults in this period were notable personalities – Ambrose, Basil, John Chrysostom, Gregory of Nazianzus (whose father was a bishop).[18] Some went further, and waited until near death before asking for baptism, by which stage it was reckoned that the risk of post-baptismal sin was minimal. The most celebrated of these 'clinical baptisms' was the Emperor Constantine himself: and the fact that after he had aligned himself with Christianity in 312 he was, though not baptized, an acceptable moderator in the disputes with the Donatists and at the Council of Nicaea, even allowing for a little tactful flexibility for the Emperor, indicates how accepted late baptism was.

At the opposite extreme leaders such as Origen and Cyprian – for the same reason, the need for the cleansing from sin that baptism offered – argued for infant baptism, lest they should die unbaptized and meet a fate which horrified the imagination. Baptism of the newborn did not wait for the great liturgical baptismal seasons when a bishop would be present. Instead they had to make do with water baptism by a priest or presbyter of the local church, and so this rite became separated from Spirit baptism, which only a bishop could properly administer. This was to lead, in the Western Church, to the division between baptism and confirmation which we know today.[19]

To begin with, for the reason described above, infant baptism was more a growing practice than an explicit doctrine, but the changing practice raised new and important theological questions. If baptism was a washing away of sin

p. 39f. References to patristic sources are given where possible to J. P. Migne. *Patrologia Graeca* (PG) or *Patrologia Latina* (PL), followed by volume and column number.

[18]See Geoffrey Wainwright, *Christian Initiation*, Lutterworth Press, 1969, p. 44f.

[19]See chapter 5, p.101.

and the start of a new life of grace, upon repentance and faith, what happened for infants? The question centred on the relationship of divine grace and human freewill, and on the bitter controversy between Augustine and Pelagius. Pelagius believed that an unqualified doctrine of human fallenness and depravity left no place for human responsibility and freedom of choice, which he saw as the good gift of the Creator. However man may fail and misuse these gifts, he begins life with them. He does not inherit original sin from his parents: he learns to sin by custom and example.

It was partly against this view that Augustine developed the principle of original sin and of infant baptism as a corollary of it, earlier propounded by Cyprian, based on a view of human nature in total contrast to that of Pelagius. On this view, he saw baptism as essential for the cleansing of the sin with which everyone is born:

Baptism washes away all, absolutely all, our sins,
whether of deed, word or thought, whether sin
original or added, whether knowingly or unknowingly
contracted.[20]

So it was that this logic – baptism seen as washing away of sin ... sin as original ... baptism as necessary for salvation ... – led to infant baptism as the universal practice, but founded it upon an understanding of baptism as centrally washing, cleansing, purifying.

---

[20]*Against Two Letters of Pelagius*, 3.2.5 (PL 44, 590), ET ed. Marcus Dods, T. & T. Clark, 1876, vol. XV, pp. 300ff. Augustine himself was not baptized in infancy, though he argues strenuously for infant baptism as the proper rule. (*Confessions*, I.11 and *Enchiridion*, 13 (PL 32, 668 and 40, 237), ET *The Library of Christian Classics*, SCM, 1955, ed. A. C. Outler, vol. VII, p. 39 and pp. 365ff.)

For 1500 years the Augustinian-Pelagian controversy has polarised belief. Heresies and controversies tend to lead to over-compensation, and the church has become so scared of anything remotely smacking of Pelagianism that it has lurched in the opposite direction. Almost by accident, the doctrine of original sin and the practice of infant baptism came to reinforce one another. Indeed the doctrine of original sin supplied the practice of baptizing infants with the theological justification it hitherto lacked, while the baptism of infants offered the church a way of dealing with the spiritual problem of original sin. And the imagery which brought both these difficult concepts vividly alive for people was the washing imagery of baptism.

Undeniably of course baptism looks like washing; baptistries and fonts are like basins or baths; and down the years that image has firmed, theologically and liturgically. In many churches, those being baptized, babes or adults, are plunged or immersed in the waters. The symbolism is vividly clear (though there is another quite different image at work here which we shall explore in the next chapter). Whatever else it may symbolise it does look like washing, making something clean. Other ancient cultures, in Africa or Asia for example, also preserve ritual washings which are part of everyday life and even of religion. And in Western culture too customs and rituals, in some ways not unlike those of ancient Israel, are carefully observed. The difference is that our modern rituals have become secularised. They take place in the home, the kitchen, the factory, the surgery, the operating theatre; bathtime is probably one of the earliest rituals any of us can remember. We know, as the writers of Leviticus knew, that these purificatory procedures have to be repeated over and over again: that indeed is the secret of their effectiveness; that is how hygiene is maintained, food kept fresh, and disease avoided, and so the health of the household and of the

35

community is safeguarded. An outbreak of salmonella poisoning calls not just for treating the victims, but tracing the problem back to its source in contaminated food or a dirty kitchen somewhere. The system has broken down, the rituals have not been observed, someone has broken the rules, and bad things happen when people grow careless.

Like the Jews we can draw from these familiar, everyday situations symbols which, though borrowing from them, actually point beyond them to something deeper about the individual personality and the quality of a society's life. So we can understand that baptism, though it looks like washing – *because* indeed it looks like washing – actually represents purifying of a different, deeper kind, which does not have to be repeated again and again but is once for all. This seems clear and easy to lay hold of. Yet many Christians (and many outside Christianity) find great difficulty in understanding what this means, and accepting the truth of it for themselves. Why is this? Is it because however recognisable the image of washing is, it is much too limited to portray the complexity and richness of baptism because it cannot express the scale and scope of the saving act of God in Christ to which baptism points? Baptism speaks not just of purification but of atonement, of the reconciliation of creature and creation to God, of the reintegration of what belongs together but has become broken, or damaged, or divided. We, and all humankind, are part of that brokenness and separation; it is a problem we inherit as newcomers to the human race. Yet the astonishing point of the Christian Gospel is that despite that, atonement – the work of putting-together-again, of reconciliation – is to involve not just God but us with God. We are not just the problem: we are part of the answer. Yet our mind, will, and spirit are so damaged that we cannot begin to take our part in dealing with the problem unless God takes the initiative. We are like a climber, trapped on a rock face, whose rescue depends on his cooperation with ropes, handholds, steps – but who can only begin to make any move at all, and to loosen his panic grip on the rock in front of him, when rescuers start to climb down to his side and then slowly lead him to safety. God takes the initiative – but not by making a conciliatory gesture, or uttering an encouraging, reassuring word from where he stands. Something much more radical and inventive is needed. God has to be our response as well, response as well as initiative, to lead us out from the trap which human nature, left to itself, had become.

To see atonement, God dealing with sin, as essentially cleansing however both diminishes the scale of atonement and narrows the thrust of baptism. It is not just a matter of 'being cleansed', for despite it we still find it too difficult to be forgiven. We would feel much better about it, much more ready to accept forgiveness, if we could take some kind of deliberate step for our part – if we could 'repent'. Our problem is not that we find it hard to confess our failure. Christians are often tempted to indulge in a catalogue of moral failures, actual or imagined, in a fashion that is not spiritual but neurotic. But to be forgiven, to accept forgiveness, we find hard, and that is probably why we can become so preoccupied with confession. We take our own (perhaps rather trivial) sins rather too seriously, because we do not take God and his gracious offer in Christ seriously enough. We do not quite know what to do with his forgiveness. We are deeply suspicious of free gifts: what is the catch? we ask. We find it easier if we have the chance to ask for it, to repent. That is by no means ruled out; our cry for help is an important aspect of our turning towards God. But repentance is at root a response, not an initiative on our part. The initiative is not ours, never was ours. It was always God's, in creation, in election, in incarnation, in suffering and

37

death, in resurrection. It is to this that baptism points – back to God in Christ reconciling the world to himself, forward to life to be lived in that reality. The repentance, the *metanoia*, the radical change of mind, is not our bold step, but our response to God's bold step taken for us, God's grace given to us in Christ, and sealed for us in baptism.

There are two major problems in this, not theoretical doctrinal problems, but pressing, painful issues which call for thoughtful pastoral care. Firstly, some of us find it hard to accept that God does not need anything from us at the start but openness – and not even the deliberate, thought-out openness of maturity, but rather the helpless openness and vulnerability of a baby. As a result, those who think like this yearn, and in some cases insist on, a reopening of the case, at least to get the chance to show that we believe God can do this for us and that we are aware of what is involved. Some who think like this demand a new baptism. Others have a different problem: we find it hard to accept that we are accepted, indeed we doubt whether we are actually acceptable. We are so doubtful of ourselves that we are incapable of receiving the gift of grace. Our guilt, our bad feelings, seem beyond casting out, and we cannot imagine letting them go and living without them. The gulf between climber and rescuer is too wide. We try, in prayer, in reflection and self-chastising, but moving out from where we are seems quite impossible. If we have been baptized as infants, we now reject that baptism. It has achieved nothing, changed nothing; if it had, we would not be trapped in this despair. It has failed the test.

Each of these very real situations in which people see themselves is at root the failure to find a gracious God. This is either because we cannot accept 'mere grace' as the basis of our relationship to him, or because we cannot accept 'mere grace' as the assurance that we *are* acceptable, that we are already pardoned. Baptism has all along been portrayed to us as the affirmation of acceptance and forgiveness, yet somehow it has not got through to us. Why this contradiction? Is it that the washing-cleansing imagery is not related to modern Christian worship or life-style in any real way, that it belongs to a religious landscape that is past and has no reality in the here and now? Or has baptism not 'got through' to us because at one and the same time it is affirmed and denied? What are we to make of the contradiction in a proclamation which at one and the same time affirms a baptism for the remission of sins, while insistently teaching a doctrine of man's worthlessless, failure, and unrelieved depravity before God? This is nothing less than to go back behind baptism, and to deny its reality in the Christian's life. J.-J. von Allmen sounds an important warning, concerning the distinction between preaching which leads from unbelief to baptism and that which leads from baptism to the Lord's table:

> ... we are in great danger of preaching as though baptism still lay, and always would lie ahead of us ... Conversion must be recalled, not proposed; the Church is to be awakened, not founded; the aim of preaching is not to make our parishioners take baptismal vows, but to insist that they confirm those vows by conduct which bears witness to them.[21]

What then is to be done about the deep anxiety which can cripple the spirit, the crushing sense of guilt, the depression, the want of any feeling of worth with which so many are left by religion? What have we to say to those who interpret and preach holiness as moral hygiene, and whose constant fear is of being contaminated by a casual lapse? The awful paradox is that the sacrament which is given to us to celebrate

[21]*Preaching and Congregation*, Lutterworth Press, 1962, p. 10f.

our liberation in Christ becomes that which insidiously questions our standing before God, and makes us doubt our freedom from the power of sin, or the validity of anything except a mature and articulate baptism of repentance. Is it surprising that some adult Christians cannot accept their infant baptism, since it seems to them to deny them the right to take their repentance into their own hands and seek by it a convincing assurance of pardon? It is then a short step to a second baptism, and to the relief of having made a deliberate confession of faith, of having received a genuine assurance, and so feeling forgiven. I suspect that so long as cleansing and washing are allowed to be the central image in baptism, in the popular mind if not in official doctrine, the logic of infant baptism will be beyond many in the church. The word is being made to call the sacrament in question.

The Good News is what we are, not what we are not:

> God was in Christ reconciling the world to himself, not counting their trespasses against them, and entrusting to us the message of reconciliation. So we are ambassadors for Christ, God making his appeal through us. We beseech you on behalf of Christ, be reconciled to God. For our sake he made him to be sin who knew no sin, so that in him we might become the righteousness of God (II Corinthians 5: 19–21).

> Do you not know that the unrighteous will not inherit the kingdom of God? . . . And such were some of you. But you were washed, you were sanctified, you were justified in the name of the Lord Jesus Christ and in the Spirit of our God (I Corinthians 6: 9–11).

The New Testament abounds in emphatic aorists. Grace is present because it is already given, has suffered, died and risen, has already reached out to us, called us, made us new.

How important it is then for preaching and worship to reassure and encourage, sending people on their way feeling 'gracious', valued, with a sense again of dignity and of worth. One of the classic sermons on this theme is by Paul Tillich:

> Grace strikes us when we are in great pain and restlessness. It strikes us when we walk through the dark valley of a meaningless and empty life. It strikes us when we feel that our separation is deeper than usual, because we have violated another life, a life which we loved, or from which we were estranged. It strikes us when our disgust for our own being, our indifference, our weakness, our hostility, and our lack of direction and composure have become intolerable to us. It strikes us when, year after year, the longed-for perfection of life does not appear, when old compulsions reign within us as they have for decades, when despair destroys all joy and courage. Sometimes at that moment a wave of light breaks into our darkness, and it is as though a voice were saying: 'You are accepted. *You are accepted*, accepted by that which is greater than you, and the name of which you do not know. Do not ask for the name now; perhaps you will find it later. Do not try to do anything now; perhaps later you will do much. Do not seek for anything; do not perform anything; do not intend anything. *Simply accept the fact that you are accepted*! If that happens to us, we experience grace. After such an experience we may not be better than before, and we may not believe more than before. But everything is transformed. In that moment, grace conquers sin, and reconciliation bridges the gulf of estrangement. And nothing is demanded of this experience, no religious or moral or intellectual presupposition, nothing but *acceptance*.[22]

Word and sacrament seal one another.

According to the Gospel, remission of sins does not mean immunity from sin; it means the removal of the power of sin to dominate and distort thinking, feeling and will.

[22] *The Shaking of the Foundations*, Penguin, 1962, p. 163f.

Repentance then is living the Christian life in that conviction, and being able to be no longer closed to the indwelling Spirit of God, nor deaf to the heavenly voice, but open, receptive, and trusting. It is to this that baptism, infant or adult, points and leads. It is this that makes it possible to deal, or to be helped to deal, with despair and a sense of worthlessness. Grace overcomes disgrace. All this is the good work of baptism. But not, I fear, if baptism is seen and taught as merely the washing away of sin. Something more, something capable of 'reaching out into wider areas of human experience, and of touching new interpretations of life' as F. R. Dillistone puts it, something more clearly radical and lifechanging, is needed.

Chapter Three

DELIVERANCE

The refreshing, sweetening, renewing qualities of water found natural expression in a complex pattern of ritual purification in Israel. Not surprisingly then, when for particular purposes a special water-rite, a 'baptism', was devised and prescribed, the outward washing was believed to signal an inward cleansing. As a result, washing or cleansing became, and has remained ever since, a powerful baptismal image for Christians. This is reflected in the Book of Acts (2:38–41, 22:16), but nothing in Acts prepares us for the startling insight and imagination with which Paul unfolds the significance of baptism for the young church. It is, he seems to say, not merely like being washed (although there is that in it); it is much more like being drowned. Plainly there is a quite different image of water at work here.

Everyone knows how dangerous and destructive water can be – a river in flood bursts its banks, a dam crumbles and a reservoir pours through; suddenly what was safely contained is out of control, sweeping down with devastating speed and force. A peaceful valley becomes a death trap; nowhere is safe, and there is no escape. That, on a *cosmic* scale, was what people in the ancient world dreaded. The cosmology that forms a background to the Old Testament was based on the belief that the universe began as a dark, watery chaos, and that it was within that that the world as they knew it was formed. The marvel of creation, as they saw it,[1] was that

[1]See e.g. B. W. Anderson, "Creation", *The Interpreter's Dictionary of the Bible*, Abingdon Press, vol. I, pp. 725ff.
Most of what we know of the Hebrew understanding of creation comes of course not from the creation accounts of Genesis 1–2 but from elsewhere

out of that primal chaos God formed the world, a safe place in which there was order and stability, light as well as darkness, dry land amidst the seas, living creatures – and man-woman, made in God's image, to live in this world, to enjoy it, and to share in the safeguarding of its rhythm, order and plenty. Like the rest of the ancient world the people of the Old Testament saw the universe as three storeyed (Exodus 20: 4, Job 26: 7–11, Psalm 148: 4–7). By his word of authority God had driven back the waters, behind the dome of the heavens (the firmament), and below the disc of the earth. The deeps beneath the earth concealed another threat – a great and terrible monster, called Rahab, or Leviathan; but such was the might and authority of God that even the monster was made to submit and banished to the depths.[2]

It was not imagined that the visible world replaced the original chaos. The seething waters were still there, held back by God's continuing command from invading the earth, but always a threat that humankind could never allow themselves, out of arrogance or carelessness, to dismiss or forget. For it was not a remote act of creation, completed once for all at the dawn of time, that the Hebrews celebrated. The world had not been established and then left to itself as a going concern. The creator God was deeply involved in the world he had fashioned. Creation was not so much an event as a relationship, a covenant between Creator and creatures. The creation accounts which are set at the beginning of the Old

in the Old Testament e.g. Job 9, 12, 37–41; Isaiah 40, 44; Psalms 8, 24, 65, 77, 89, 93, 95, 104, 136, 148, etc.

[2]Psalm 74: 12–14, 89: 8–11, 104: 25–26; Job 26: 12–24, 41: 1–11.

See Rabbi Shalom M. Paul, "Creation and Cosmogony", *Encyclopaedia Judaica*, Keter Publishing House, Jerusalem, 1972, vol. 5, pp. 1059ff. In Genesis 1:21 there is a specific reference to the creation of 'great sea-monsters'. The Bible repudiates the ancient belief in an eternal struggle between God and the sea-monster which was the symbol of chaos. Monsters are creatures, not rival gods.

Testament only make sense in the light of the Story which then begins to unfold.

The Old Testament shows no interest in mere cosmology, no curiosity about the physical world for its own sake; that kind of observing and exploring that we are familiar with does not figure at all in its outlook. Such cosmology as we do find is really theology. The importance of the world is not that it is there, but that it is God's creation, the theatre of his dealings with humanity, and of a particular people's struggle to understand and obey the calling they believe they have from him. The Creator is the God of Abraham, and of Isaac, and of Jacob, the God of exodus and wilderness and promised land. It is the God of history, the God of their people's story, who is the Lord of creation. Even more astonishingly, they discovered, the God who brought order out of chaos and life out of emptiness is he to whom they could cry 'my God', in despair or in delight, for he was also the one who heard the individual's prayer, pardoned each one's sins, and led this one and that from darkness to light. It is in fact in those sections of the Old Testament where faith and life are most deeply and adventurously reflected on and wrestled with that there are most references to creation and the creator God. In Job, and even more in the Psalms, there are rich seams of thought and imagination as people attempted to understand both the majesty and the nearness of God, and how majesty and nearness are interrelated. The image of the waters and their mastery which we have seen to be the central symbol of creation is used in praise of the might of the Creator (24: 1–2, 29: 1–11, 33: 6–9, 93: 3–4, 95: 4–5, 96: 10–13, 98: 7–9, 104: 1–9, 136: 1–6, 13–15, 148: 4ff), in affirmation of confidence in God (46: 1–3, 65: 5–10, 69: 1–2, 13–15) in thankfulness for deliverance from enemies (18: 4–19, 42: 6–8), and in appeal to God to show again his might as of old (74: 12–14, 77: 11–20; see also Job 9: 1–10, 26: 1–14, 38:

4–11; Proverbs 8: 22–31; Isaiah 8: 5–8, 43: 1–2, 54: 7–10). 'The waters' came to be a figure for anything that threatened to undermine or destroy what was good and God-given – an intimidating enemy, national or personal, or the collapse of a kingdom, or a disastrous harvest, or, more subtly, unfaithfulness and unrighteousness flooding through everything and everyone in a decadent, corrupt regime.

As we have seen, it is crucial to the Old Testament understanding of life in the created world that stability and safety cannot be taken for granted. Alongside the story of creation stands the story of the flood. The orderliness of creation is maintained by the creator's word. The fiat of Genesis 1 does not merely bring the world into being: it holds it in being, keeping back the waters above and beneath (cf. Jeremiah 4: 23–28, 5: 22f). Creation can be unmade:

> In the six hundredth year of Noah's life, in the second month, on the seventeenth day of the month, on that day all the foundations of the great deep burst forth, and the windows of the heavens were opened. And rain fell upon the earth forty days and forty nights (Genesis 7: 11–12; cf. 6: 6–7, 11–13).

Yet the outcome of this disaster is not a return to chaos, but a reaffirmation of creation, and a renewal of the gracious covenant which is at the heart of creation:

> And God said, 'This is the sign of the covenant which I make between me and you and every living creature that is with you, for all future generations: I set my bow in the cloud and it shall be a sign of the covenant between me and the earth. When I bring clouds over the earth and the bow is seen in the clouds, I will remember my covenant which is between me and you and every living creature of all flesh; and the waters shall never again become a flood to destroy all flesh'. (Genesis 9: 12–15).[3]

[3]Tertullian described the Flood as 'the baptism of the world' – *On*

The waters, the abyss of Genesis, remain however as part of the picture. The abyss is the place of oblivion, of forgottenness, of ultimate destruction (Psalm 69: 1–2, 14–15, 88: 14–18, 130: 1), yet not beyond the reach of God's hand, as the book of Jonah neatly explains. Even this disobedient man, who in his desperation actually runs away to sea, of all places, and, worse, is actually swallowed by a great fish (Leviathan?), calls from the fish in the deep to God, and is heard and rescued – how much more will God reach and rescue the people of Nineveh!

It is clear then that the image of water as danger and threat, and as the setting for deliverance, is a major theme in the Old Testament. A primitive idea is explored and developed so that it expresses not only the instinctive sense of menace that might be commonplace in ancient minds, but something more, something original and without parallel in any other culture then or since. The image of the waters speaks of the faithfulness and steadfast love of God, of a cosmic authority, pointing not just to the reliability of the world and the place humankind is given in it, but also to the possibility of faith and hope *even when things go wrong*. This is the ground of a theology of crisis, global, corporate, and individual, ultimately to be expressed in the cross, but already germinating in the Old Testament. Passing through the waters can mean not death but life; it can lead not to annihilation but to salvation. Through the waters wrong can be put right, righteousness vindicated, the wicked punished, and God's faithful ones borne to safety.

How did that Old Testament theme become linked to baptism? It is hard to escape the conclusion that it was Jesus who himself made the connection. It is this image of water,

---

Baptism, 8 (PL 1, 1316), op. cit. p. 19. Note too the use made of the imagery of the Flood and the rescue in I Peter 3: 18–21.

the dark primeval element, that must be the clue to the significance of the important sayings of Jesus about his 'baptism'. These sayings occur at two places, Mark 10: 35–40 and Luke 12: 49–50:

> James and John, the sons of Zebedee, came forward to him and said to him, 'Teacher, we want you to do for us whatever we ask of you'. And he said to them, 'What do you want me to do for you?' And they said to him, 'Grant us to sit, one at your right hand and one at your left, in your glory'. But Jesus said to them, 'You do not know what you are asking. Are you able to drink the cup that I drink, or to be baptized with the baptism with which I am baptized?' And they said to him, 'We are able'. And Jesus said to them, 'The cup that I drink you will drink; and with the baptism with which I am baptized you will be baptized; but to sit at my right hand or at my left is not mine to grant, but it is for those for whom it has been prepared'.

> I came to cast fire upon earth; and would that it were already kindled! I have a baptism to be baptized with; and how I am constrained until it is accomplished!

Such vivid sayings have naturally been the centre of scholarly controversy. There is strong support for considering them original sayings of Jesus. Vincent Taylor says:

> ... there is no reason to suppose that current sacramental practice has influenced the form of the saying. On the contrary, it is more justly interpreted as an original and creative utterance ... (A contrary view) too narrowly interprets the saying as a prophecy of martyrdom ... martyrdom is not exclusively meant or even necessarily implied, for the NT does not use the imagery of baptism in this sense, and it is not found in Christian usage until the turn of the second century.[4]

[4] *The Gospel according to Mark*, Macmillan, 1953, p. 441. See also Eduard Schweizer, *The Good News according to Mark*, SPCK, 1971, p. 218; *The*

To what do these sayings refer? Why does Jesus speak of what is to come as his '*baptism*'? If the baptism in Jordan at the hands of John was the deeply meaningful event that the evangelists describe it to have been, then these sayings of Jesus must be somehow related to it. That baptism is seen in the Gospels however as an event that had yet to be fully explained. The significance that was becoming uppermost was not merely or mainly the washing and the *metanoia*, the turning to face a new direction, even though, as we saw, that was not as inappropriate for Jesus as is sometimes alleged. It was the action of undergoing baptism, the going down into the waters and coming through and up from the waters, that was so telling and so abidingly important for him. That was when the heavens had opened, and the voice had spoken, and the dove had descended; and that was when Jesus recognised and received his ministry, his role as obedient Son and suffering servant. (Matthew 3: 16–17; Mark 1: 10; Luke 3: 21–22). So his baptism, in the sense in which it is spoken of in Mark and Luke, lay both in the past and in the future; it was both completed and yet still unfulfilled. It meant what he looked back to – the immersing, the voice, the descending Spirit – and *therefore also* what he now saw ahead – another kind of submitting, accepting, going down and into and through. 'The baptism of Jesus is thus much more than the initial event marking the beginning of his ministry. Implicit in it is the basic pattern of his vocation'.[5]

He was himself baptized by John the Baptist and this is presented as the prime fact in the commencement of his

Good News according to Luke, SPCK, 1984, p. 215; Howard Marshall, *The Gospel of Luke*, The Paternoster Press, 1978, p. 547.
[5]Elmer J. F. Arndt, *The Font and the Table*, Lutterworth Press, 1967, p. 38.

ministry. There must have been many other firsts in the growing life of a child towards manhood, which have not been recorded because theologically less significant, but the Baptism is treated in the Gospels with considerable detail. His Baptism, with his whole life, is the willing 'Amen' of Jesus to the purposes of the Father, for which as Son of God, Son of Mary, he had come into the world. He is Messiah both in virtue of the Father's sending, and also by his own acceptance in obedience of all that sending involved. So in sharing with those whom John called to make ready for the coming rule of God by baptism in the Jordan, Jesus initiates his own mission, and regards that baptism of John as being filled out and fulfilled, up to his death upon the Cross. He "interpreted his whole life and ministry thereafter as the Baptism with which he was being baptized, and identified its fulfilment with his passion and death upon the Cross".[6]

The point of the sayings about baptism in Mark and Luke is still further sharpened when we notice the context in which they are set. In Mark: 'They were on the road going to Jerusalem, and Jesus was walking ahead of them: and they were amazed, and those who followed were afraid . . .' (Mark 10: 32). Jesus then speaks of impending opposition, suffering and death, and this is the point at which the sons of Zebedee ask about places in the kingdom, bypassing the question of discipleship and reaching beyond to achievement and reward. Their request seems quite unconnected to what has just been said; Jesus then makes them see the connection – 'You do not know what you are asking . . .' – and then follow the images of cup and baptism. Life in the kingdom is distant and uncertain. Too much still lies in the way. All that is certain as

[6]Report of the Panel of Doctrine, *Church of Scotland General Assembly Reports 1983*, p. 154, quoting from an earlier report, *The Doctrine of Baptism*, The Saint Andrew Press, 1966. See also G. W. H. Lampe, *The Seal of the Spirit*, Longmans Green & Co., 1951, pp. 38ff.

yet is that there will be suffering and death, cup and baptism. In Luke 12 the baptism saying occurs towards the end of a section of teaching about the imminence and unpredictability of the end, and about the importance of faithful discipleship, come what may – the obedience and faithfulness that Jesus himself was already displaying. We should not forget that the mission of John too led to imprisonment and death: in him too the symbol of the Jordan waters pointed on for the Baptizer to the ultimate baptism of death in obedience to him who called him to be the voice that cried 'Prepare the way!'

The suffering, dying and rising of Jesus is not then to be understood as 'a kind of baptism'. It is The Baptism, taking the rite of immersion, in whatever sense people knew it, and giving it powerful new substance and significance. The Baptism of dying and rising does not discard the baptism in Jordan as no longer important. On the contrary, Jesus' sayings concerning baptism give new meaning to the Jordan experience, linking it to a new baptismal image which was even more deeply embedded in the Old Testament imagination than that of washing. What was merely water baptism, signifying perhaps purification, now points to something we noted in certain of the Psalms – an immersion in utter submission, powerlessness, 'passion' in its classic sense, in the deep darkness, the empty meaninglessness, and the oblivion of the abyss. This is the baptism he 'must be baptized with'.

We see little sign that the church in Acts saw baptism in this sense, as death and deliverance. It certainly stood for forgiveness, remission, even entry into the church, *made possible* because of Christ's death and resurrection and the gift of the Spirit; but the rite that testified to this was apparently a rite of washing and cleansing. It was Paul, so far as we can see, who recognised the radical connection between Christ's death and resurrection and the Christian life through baptism.

Did he know the sayings of Jesus recorded by Mark and Luke?

The central text in Paul's thinking about baptism is Romans 6. This passage is really about law and grace, and what the decisive act of God in Christ means for Christian living. Baptism is introduced as an argument for accepting the reality of salvation in Christ, and so the call to live the new life made possible by Christ:

> What shall we say then? Are we to continue in sin that grace may abound? By no means! How can he who died to sin still live in it? Do you not know that all of us who have been baptized into Christ Jesus were baptized into his death? We were buried therefore with him by baptism into death, so that as Christ was raised from the dead by the glory of the Father, we too might walk in newness of life. For if we have been united with him in a death like his, we shall certainly be united with him in a resurrection like his. We know that our old self was crucified with him so that the sinful body might be destroyed, and we might no longer be enslaved to sin. For he who has died is freed from sin. But if we have died with Christ, we believe that we shall also live with him. For we know that Christ being raised from the dead will never die again, death no longer has dominion over him. The death he died he died to sin, once for all, but the life he lives he lives to God. So you also must consider yourselves dead to sin and alive to God in Christ Jesus (Romans 6: 1–11).

Paul appeals to baptism as the conclusive sign that we are incorporate 'in Christ'. We have 'died with Christ' but we are now 'alive in Christ'; in Christ we are 'dead to sin', and 'alive to God'; and the sign of all this is baptism. But if he uses baptism to explain that we are 'in Christ', and to bring home to his readers what that means, then he must have been able to assume that such a logic was at least recognisable to them. Nor is this by any means an isolated reference. In other letters, in various contexts, in answer to the questions and needs of his congregations in widely contrasting circumstances, Paul uses the theme of baptism as a cornerstone of his theology (I Cor. 1: 12–17, Gal. 3: 26–28, Eph. 4: 1–6, Col. 2: 8–15). In order to clear up a confusion in the minds of his readers, Paul can point to the fact that they were baptized, as it were to settle the matter. They were baptized – that was agreed – and given that they could scarcely deny the logic of what followed.

New Testament scholars have generally believed that the dying and rising motif which came to be associated with baptism, and which Paul uses in Romans and elsewhere, has its source in the mystery religions of the ancient world, around which widespread popular beliefs had grown. Common to many of these was a myth of a dying and rising god who was celebrated in the rites, and especially in the initiation rites, of these cults. Associated with this was a belief that by a sort of sacramental union the initiate shared in the dying and rising of the god. Such beliefs, in one form or another, were so common across the ancient world of the New Testament period that it might have been natural for Paul, a masterly image-builder, to draw upon them to illustrate the significance of Christian baptism and to develop the range of its meaning – perhaps even to set it over against the mystery cults as the real contrasted with the sham. According to this view it is as if Paul were saying, "Everyone knows about 'dying and rising', the pagan cults are full of it. But you know (Romans 6: 3, 6) that for us dying and rising mean that something far greater, far more profound, has happened. Christ has really died, once for all, and has really risen (Romans 6: 10–11), and therefore we may 'set our feet upon the new path of life', and regard ourselves as 'dead to sin and alive to God, in union with Christ Jesus' ".

Others however are sceptical about this.[7] They argue that

to trace the baptism teaching of Paul, or of those who continued his thinking, in Romans, Corinthians, Colossians etc, to the mystery cults is not only mistaken but seriously misleading, because it tends to blur the distinctiveness of what Paul expounds. The centre of Paul's argument in Romans 6, and in the other comparable passages, is the 'once-for-all-ness' of the death of Jesus. It is to this that baptism points; it is this indeed that baptism joyfully celebrates.

> . . . the tension between a death with Christ at Golgotha and a death with him in baptism perhaps becomes more comprehensible.

> When the new convert is baptized, he does not act out the death and resurrection of Jesus by going below the water and coming up out of it again in imitation of Jesus. Rather, when Jesus was crucified the old humanity was crucified with him (verse 6) and when a man in faith accepts God's justification and offers himself for baptism this is his appropriation of what Christ has done – his acceptance of it as done for himself. As a result his *feet* are *set . . . upon the new path of life.*[8]

There are in the developing understanding of baptism no doubt echoes of the Graeco-Roman mysteries which so pervaded the popular imagination of those times. These might have helped to provide a frame of reference for Christians as they reflected on what Paul wrote. But had these cults and their myths been the only basis for the great deliverance image of baptism the church would surely have given it a wide berth: the dangers of slipping into paganism were only

[7]See e.g. Ernest Best, *The Letter of Paul to the Romans*, Cambridge University Press, 1967, p. 68, and A. J. M. Wedderburn, *Baptism and Resurrection: Studies in Pauline Theology against its Graeco-Roman Background*, J. C. B. Mohr (Paul Siebeck), Tubingen, 1987.

[8]Best, op. cit. p. 67; see also Wedderburn, op. cit. p. 66.

too well known and feared. The Christian Gospel had something new to say, and it was Paul's genius that he grasped the connection between that once-for-all dying and rising that was the Gospel's centre and the rite of baptism which incorporated the new Christian into it:

> . . . the roots of such language lie in the idea, so pervasive in the Old Testament and Judaism, of the involvement of subsequent generations in the earlier actions of a representative figure or figures, and in the solidarity of a race with one another down through history. But now, in Paul's thought, the earlier generation has shrunk to but one figure, the eschatological human being, Christ, and the race has broadened to the whole of humanity. That one person died and with him all for whom he died; that past death is declared afresh in baptism, as the baptized says her or his 'Amen' to the past representative act, pledging herself or himself to live henceforth in solidarity both with the representative and all those represented by him; at the same time she or he receives the promise of new life uttered in the vindication of that same representative person by his resurrection from the dead.[9]

Did Paul know the baptism sayings of Jesus recorded by Mark and Luke? Whether he did or not must remain a matter of speculation. There is certainly no parallel for baptism to the teaching regarding the Supper he speaks of having 'received' at I Corinthians 11: 23ff. Yet the strength and credibility of Paul's baptismal teaching lies in the fact that, however it came about, it goes back behind the teaching reflected in Acts and provides the needed connection between Christian baptism and the sayings relating to it which are recorded in the Gospels.[10]

[9]Wedderburn, p. 395f.
[10]See Lampe op. cit., p. 52f: "St. Paul need not have looked outside the

Closely linked to the dying-rising view of baptism is that of 'newness'. It is this that baptism leads to:

> We were buried therefore with him by baptism into death, so that as Christ was raised from the dead by the glory of the Father, we too might walk in newness of life (Romans 6: 4)

> For as many of you as were baptized into Christ have put on Christ. There is neither Jew nor Greek, there is neither slave nor free, there is neither male nor female; for you are all one in Christ Jesus (Galatians 3: 27–28)

To have been baptized into Christ – to be in Christ therefore – is to have undergone a radical change, to have moved from one life to another. The new status, the new life that it opens up, means in turn new relationships to one another, often cutting across the divisions and the gradings within which people still have to live in the community. Baptism proclaims that we can live the new life in the midst of the old (I Corinthians: 12–13). Baptism has this decisive quality because it proclaims for each new Christian the decisiveness of Christ's death and resurrection. Indeed it means 'a reenactment for the believer of what once happened to our Lord', says Flemington:

> primitive tradition for the basic elements in his mystical theology, though it required his personal experience and spiritual insight to enable the Church to arrive at a conscious realisation of much that it had previously perceived but dimly ... St. Paul's teaching does not represent a wholly new conception of Baptism; it consists largely in the explicit and detailed presentation in the light of his profound personal experience of what had been implied in the words and actions of Jesus and in the primitive preaching. It is significant that what he brings before his converts as the foundation and focus of Christian living is not his private revelation on the Damascus road, but the initiation which they, no less than he, had received in the already existing society of the Church".

St. Paul looks back to baptism as that which marked for each Christian the inauguration of the New Age, the transition from the old life to the new. Everything began for the convert when he came up out of the water and robed himself afresh in his garments. It was really nothing less than a putting on of Christ. By that act he came to share in all the privileges of the new life; he was an heir, he was free, he was a son. He received the Spirit, and heard in his own heart the echo of the very cry which Jesus uttered in his moment of closest communion with God.[11]

Flemington, citing also Vincent Taylor, suggests that Paul 'rarely links baptism with forgiveness'. Vincent Taylor refers to 'the deliberate preference of Paul for the idea of justification, which he rightly believed to be a much richer conception than forgiveness as he knew it and understood it'.[12] In the Synoptic Gospels and Acts however, as we have seen, repentance and forgiveness of sins figure prominently in what is said and understood of baptism. The marked contrast between these two approaches to baptism seems to indicate that they are not really compatible with one another, and that they present us with two fundamentally different understandings of baptism, one essentially subjective, and the other objective, one which centres baptism on our response to God in repentance and faith, and the other which centres baptism on God's action in Christ for us. Putting it like that to some extent distorts the contrast: repentance is of course the individual's answer to what God has done in Christ; likewise, no account of the dying and rising of Christ can leave out the fact of forgiveness in Christ. Nevertheless too much is blurred by merely merging the distinctiveness of a subjective and an objective understanding into one another.

[11]op. cit., p. 73.
[12]"Constructive Theology 1. – Forgiveness", *Expository Times*, vol. 51, 1939–40, pp. 16–21.

The deliverance image of baptism appears again in I Peter, which is usually considered to be a baptismal homily. In chapter 3 there is a word picture in which baptism is likened to the rescue of the crew and passengers of the ark:

> For Christ also died for sins once for all, the righteous for the unrighteous, that he might bring us to God, being put to death in the flesh but made alive in the spirit; in which he went and preached to the spirits in prison, who formerly did not obey, when God's patience waited in the days of Noah, during the building of the ark, in which a few, that is, eight persons, were saved through water. Baptism, which corresponds to this, now saves you, not as a removal of dirt from the body but as an appeal to God for a clear conscience, through the resurrection of Jesus Christ, who has gone into heaven and is at the right hand of God, with angels, authorities, and powers subject to him. (I Peter 3: 18–22).

If that was indeed part of the sermon at a service of baptism how dramatic the words 'baptism now saves you' must have sounded to the nervous but excited candidates as the great moment approached; and how plainly they express the 'objective' view of baptism discussed above.

It has been pointed out[13] that words referring to 'suffering' turn up with marked frequency in I Peter. *pascho* appears twelve times here, yet only seven times in all the Pauline epistles, and four in Hebrews. *pathema* occurs four times in I Peter, compared with ten times in the rest of the epistles. If we accept that I Peter is closely concerned with baptism and with the teaching of those about to be baptized, then it looks as if baptism was linked to suffering in the minds of Christians in that situation. Here therefore is another exposition of the dying-rising baptism image which we have traced in Paul, this

[13]F. L. Cross, *I Peter: a Paschal Liturgy*, Mowbray & Co., 1954, pp. 15ff.

time from a quite different source. So it offers additional
evidence that a sophisticated and developed understanding of
baptism as deliverance through the dying and rising of Christ
was to be found in the church, especially associated with
major figures among the church's leaders; yet there is virtually
no sign of such thinking and teaching in the records of Acts.
We must of course beware of overstating what can only be
conjectured, and of claiming to see hints of baptism in all
sorts of places, likely or unlikely, throughout the New
Testament. Yet we have seen that baptism must have been a
central feature of the life of the church – at least as central as
the eucharist. And baptism does begin to look like a lens
through which, once correctly focussed, we can see more
clearly how the church came to understand and live the
Christian life in the midst of great uncertainty and threat.

A thorough trace of baptismal doctrine and images through
the period of the early church is beyond the scope of these
lectures. It is however possible to see that although the image
of washing with an emphasis on baptism as forgiveness and
renewal became central again, in the thinking of the Fathers,
the deliverance understanding was by no means lost to view.
Indeed there are indications at times of a continuing tension
between the forgiveness and the deliverance motifs, the
subjective and the objective views of baptism, which we have
already noted in the New Testament. Cyril of Jerusalem,
delivering his Catechetical Lectures to candidates for baptism,
around 350 – speaking actually in the Church of the Holy
Sepulchre – sets the two paradigms we have outlined against
one another:

> Let no one then suppose that baptism is merely the grace of
> remission of sins, or further, that of adoption; as John's
> baptism bestowed only the remission of sins. Nay we know
> full well, that as it purges our sins, and conveys to us the gift

of the Holy Spirit, so also it is the counterpart of Christ's sufferings. For, for this cause Paul, just now read, cried aloud and says, 'Know ye not that as many of us as were baptized into Christ Jesus, were baptized into his death? Therefore we are buried with him by baptism into death' (Rom. 6: 3). These words he spoke to them who had settled with themselves that baptism ministers to us the remission of sins, and adoption; but not that further it has communion also in representation with Christ's true sufferings.[14]

And Theodore of Mopsuestia, setting out his baptismal teaching around 400 wrote:

When I am baptized and my head is immersed, I receive the death of the Lord and I wish to receive his burial; and I thereby profess my belief in the resurrection of our Lord, for I think when I am come out of the water that I have already risen, symbolically as it were.[15]

Such extracts from baptismal teaching in the late fourth and early fifth centuries confirm that the identification of baptism, by vivid imagery, with the death and resurrection of Christ had not been lost. Indeed because of this, baptism took on a particular importance in the early church in times of persecution. Preparation for baptism could take several years. If during that time a catechumen was imprisoned for his beliefs, he could be baptized without further delay; if he was put to death while still a catechumen and before being baptized, that was considered to have been his baptism; he had undergone a real, and not merely a symbolic, baptism. Martyrdom, 'baptism of blood', was the fulfilment of the Lord's words, 'with the baptism with which I am baptized

---

[14]*Catechetical Lectures*, 20.6 (PG 33, 1081), ET in *A Library of the Fathers*, vol. II, Parker, 1839, p. 265.

[15]*Homilies*, 14.5.

you will be baptized', and the disciple who followed along that way would share not only the death but also the resurrection to which it led.

All this would be dramatically clear for Christians in time of hostility and persecution. It would still have obvious meaning while converts were being won over from paganism in large numbers. Gradually however this flow of the adult converts who became first generation Christians slowed down, and baptism centred more and more on the children of parents who were already baptized. Perhaps in part because of this there was a theological shift, and as infant baptism increasingly became the norm the stress seems to have moved to regeneration and purification. Later, in the medieval church, the theme of dying and deliverance became lost: there was, as one writer says, 'nothing to be delivered from or to – it had already happened by birth'. But in a famous passage Luther writes:

Baptism, then, signifies two things – death and resurrection, that is, full and complete justification. When the minister immerses the child in the water it signifies death, and when he draws it forth again it signifies life ... It is therefore indeed correct to say that baptism is a washing away of sin, but the expression of it is too mild and weak to bring out the full significance of baptism, which is rather a symbol of death and resurrection. . . . For as long as we live we are continually doing that which baptism signifies, that is, we die and rise again ... We must therefore beware of those who have reduced the power of baptism to such small and slender dimensions that, while they say grace is indeed inpoured by it, they maintain that afterwards it is poured out again through sin, and that then one must reach heaven by another way, as if baptism had now became entirely useless. Do not hold such a view, but understand that this is the significance of baptism, that through it you die and live again.[16]

[16]*On the Babylonian Captivity of the Church*, "Concerning the Sacrament

Baptism had that significance for the early church and perhaps for the Reformation church too, because water, as we have seen, had powerful and deep-seated associations of danger and destruction in the common imagination of those days. Can baptism bear such an image any longer, now that children are taught to swim and enjoy water from infancy, and water has become a playground for surf-boarders, scuba-divers, water-skiers, and all who go down to the sea in ships for the fun of it? It would seem that the waters hold few terrors for modern man. Yet the huge box-office for a film, running to several sequels, about a monster shark which terrorises a Long Island holiday resort shows that Leviathan still has the power to haunt us. (Scots however have the superior cunning to give the local monster a nickname and market it (her?) as a tourist attraction, all the more appealing since no-one ever actually catches sight of the mysterious denizen).

Every age and society has its abyss and its monster, and somewhere in the collective imagination of humankind the images of terror and menace are still those of being overwhelmed, immersed, and destroyed.[17] In some respects what we today call (significantly) 'space', the vast, dark, unpredictable, essentially hostile environment in which our galaxy is set, is for us what the 'abyss', the 'void', was for people of Biblical times. In other respects it is our 'inner space' that holds for us the terror of the bottomless deep, the unknown, the short step from oblivion. Nor is it too fanciful to suggest that our Leviathan is man-made, lurking deep in the waters waiting its chance to launch such devastating wrath that it would destroy most of life as we know it upon the

of Baptism", *Works*, ed. A. R. Wentz, Muhlenberg Press, Philadelphia 1959, vol. 36. II, pp. 67ff.
[17]See Dillistone, op. cit., pp. 187ff.

earth. In this most adept and sophisticated of any generation the fear of helplessness, of being overwhelmed, is as real as ever it was, and the Psalms of fear and despair speak eloquently to us and for us still. The dangers, the 'enemies', are perhaps different, but we describe them in terms that echo the cries and prayers of the Old Testament. If baptism is to speak authentically to what threatens, frightens, and destroys, then it must in our day speak to all this, in the image of poured water. Its primary concern is not with religious dangers, not even with religious failings. Its context is the reality of life in God's world now – the political, economic, scientific, or psychological structures within which life is lived. It is at this level of experience and reality that baptism must operate. Perhaps indeed our age is able to recapture a sense of the cosmic dimension of living within which in the Biblical witness both fear and faith are set, not just as they concern our inner peace, nor even the relations between us and others, but our relation to the cosmos to whom the creator has bound us in an awe-inspiring responsibility. It is at this level of experience and reality that baptism must operate sacramentally, proclaiming grace, justification, deliverance and new life. We still participate in the baptism of Christ's incarnation, suffering, dying and rising. Life is shot through with baptismal meaning; it is a succession of dying and risings, small and great.

W. F. Flemington calls baptism 'the kerygma in action'.[18] It speaks precisely to this hazardous, anxious prospect we face with the message of hope and victory in Christ. This does not merely mean that we can therefore have confidence in face of danger, as if baptism were simply a cheering message that all will somehow be well. Because it is participation *in the dying and rising* of Christ, baptism sets us

[18]op. cit., p. 73.

free to endanger ourselves, our values, our reputation, our
theology even, and ultimately our very life, like Christ – in
Christ indeed – so as to go down alongside the helpless, the
overwhelmed, the powerless, in all manner of circumstances
like Christ, in Christ. Baptism is not only the kerygma in
action. It is what Geoffrey Wainwright calls 'the acted
response to the kerygma'.[19] It is, then, not only and not
primarily the justification of the Christian; it is the calling of
the Christian. In a report published by the Evangelical
Reformed Church of the Canton of Bern, Switzerland, there
is this claim:

> The acceptance and liberation promised in principle to all
> human beings in baptism must, (furthermore), take shape in
> the life of the church in general. The responsibility of the
> church for those who are baptized, as for those who are not,
> is also a political responsibility. It will express itself above all
> in solidarity with those who are disadvantaged in society, in
> the struggle for more justice and a better quality of life.
> Baptism should always be an impetus to change the world
> into which children are baptized according to God's will to
> redeem and liberate.[20]

It is said, with characteristic vigour, by Bonhoeffer in one
of his last letters from prison dated July 18, 1944:

> Man is challenged to participate in the sufferings of God at
> the hands of a godless world.

> He must therefore plunge himself into the life of a godless
> world, without attempting to gloss over its ungodliness with
> a veneer of religion or trying to transfigure it. He must live a

[19]*Doxology*, Epworth Press, 1980, p. 138f.
[20]"Power and Baptism", *International Review of Mission*, vol. 69, no. 273,
January 1980, p. 87.

'worldly' life and so participate in the suffering of God. He *may* live a 'worldly' life as one emancipated from all false religions and obligations. To be a Christian does not mean to be religious in a particular way, to cultivate some particular form of asceticism (as a sinner, a penitent or a saint), but to be a man. It is not some religious act which makes a Christian what he is, but participation in the suffering of God in the life of the world.

This is *metanoia*. It is not in the first instance bothering about one's own needs, problems, sins, and fears, but allowing oneself to be caught up in the way of Christ, into the Messianic event, and thus fulfilling Isaiah 53.[21]

The Christian's calling therefore is to enter into the baptism of Christ. 'Plunge ourselves into life' is a baptismal image. It is possible to live like this because Jesus has lived like this, and died like this, and from this has risen in life. We shall return to this theme in chapter 5.

Frank Lake is his *Clinical Theology* says this about baptism:

As with all biblical truths there is a paradox here. It is in the floods that deliverance comes, not when the flood has subsided. Therefore the outsider, whose only concept of cure is a total absence of tension, suffering, and conflict, cannot see the miracle that has happened. The sufficient evidence is God's Presence, revealed in the suffering. This quite changes its character for the sufferer. It becomes actually good and meaningful to him.[22]

God is not just in the rescue: he is in the danger also. The dangers are real, not just symbolic, and in God alone is the clash of good and evil, creation and destruction, life and

[21]*Letters and Papers from Prison*, SCM, 1963, p. 166.
[22]*Clinical Theology*, Darton, Longman and Todd, 1966, p. 803. See also Howard Marshall, *The Gospel of Luke*, p. 547, and G. B. Caird, *Saint Luke*, Penguin, 1963, p. 167.

death, resolved. It is this daring conviction that baptism celebrates. We may forget it, fall away from it, disbelieve it for a time, but even in these waters of doubt, failure, and utter despair there is deliverance:

> We are afflicted in every way, but not crushed; perplexed, but not driven to despair; persecuted, but not forsaken; struck down, but not destroyed; always carrying in the body the death of Jesus, so that the life of Jesus may also be manifested in our bodies. For while we live we are always being given up to death for Jesus' sake, so that the life of Jesus may be manifested in our mortal flesh (II Corinthians 4: 8–11).

Chapter Four

BIRTH

From the violent imagery of the flood and the storm to that of the quiet bustle of the labour ward seems a long way. Here everything seems calm, routine even, completely under control. Even the mother about to give birth has learned what to expect and what to do. But to one present it is very different. To one, something cataclysmic is happening, the whole world heaving, uncontrollably, alarmingly. I mean of course the babe who is being born, 'delivered', for the shift from the storm to the birth is only from one scale to another; being born is one of the most violent experiences we will ever undergo. Propelled from one world to another, from one kind of life to another, from the warm protectedness of the enfolding womb into the alien, dazzlingly bright vastness of the outside world, may well at first feel more than anything else like death, not a beginning but an ending. It is not death of course, it is life; but life can sometimes seem more frightening and threatening than death. In a broadcast interview Frank Lake once said: 'What people fear about their death is that it will be just like their birth'.

What baptism means and points to is so life-changing, such a drastic beginning, that it has always seemed right to think of it as a kind of birth, like 'being born again'. That image comes of course from the Fourth Gospel, chapter 3. This profound and difficult chapter has been enlisted in many theological causes, and almost any interpretation of it is likely to say too much for one reader, too little for another. If however it does not explicitly mention baptism it certainly has important baptismal allusions, and specifically it links baptism to the idea of birth:

> Jesus answered (Nicodemus), 'Truly, truly, I say unto you, unless one is born anew, he cannot see the kingdom of God'. Nicodemus said to him, 'How can a man be born when he is old? Can he enter a second time into his mother's womb and be born?' Jesus answered, 'Truly, truly, I say to you, unless one is born of water and the spirit, he cannot enter the kingdom of God' (John 3: 3–5).

The word *anōthen*, translated (RSV, NEB, TEV) 'anew', also, and perhaps more likely, means 'from above' (Jerusalem Bible). It is used in that sense elsewhere in John (3: 31, 19: 11, 23), and in that sense offers some explanation of Nicodemus' perplexity (v. 4). Behind this passage lies the teaching of ch. 1, that Jesus himself had been 'born from above' (1: 14–18), and 'of water and the Spirit'. At his baptism the descending Spirit testified to his true identity (1: 32–34), and Matthew, Mark and Luke tell also of a voice which said "This is my beloved son". These words echo Psalm 2: 7, which holds together both kingship and sonship, bestowed by God on his appointed servant. Like Mark 10: 38ff and Luke 12: 50, John 3 points back to the baptism by John the Baptist; and like the Synoptic sayings, this points forward to the suffering and death to which the path of the servant Son leads. "No one has ascended into heaven but he who descended from heaven, the Son of Man. And as Moses lifted up the serpent in the wilderness, so must the Son of man be lifted up" (vv. 13–14). Rebirth, birth from above, comes through the one who has himself first been born from above and has been lifted up in crucifixion. Rebirth comes through the birth, life, death, and rising of the Son of man, who is 'firstborn among many brethren' (Romans 8: 29). It is through suffering and death that new life comes. For John, birth, dying, and rising are inextricably interwoven. Once again baptism is expounded in terms of suffering.

... baptism as a life-giving rite arises out of and depends upon the incarnation and death of the heavenly Man. . . .

The truth (in John's view) seems to be that they (the sacraments) hang not upon one particular moment or command, but upon the whole fact of Christ in his life, death, and exaltation, and that they convey nothing less than this whole fact.[1]

Elsewhere in the Johannine writings this association of baptism, birth and salvation is further developed, and signs of baptismal imagery and meaning can be traced. In I John much use is made of the expression 'children of God' to describe the church, the believers, and so the baptized. (I John 3: 1–2, 4: 7–10, 5: 4–8). This imagery abounds in Paul's writings, notably in Romans 8, which follows out the consequences of being baptized in Christ of chapter 6. To be children of God, the baptized, carries with it the consequence that "we suffer with (Christ) in order that we may also be glorified with him" (Romans 8: 17).

Broadly, in the New Testament baptism is related to birth as an image of beginnings, rather than as another water image. In the writings of the Fathers however there are to be found striking, if at times somewhat eccentric, examples of birth described in terms of coming 'through the waters'. Cyril of Jerusalem (c. 350) linked the image of birth to that of dying and rising:

You have plunged thrice in the water, and have come forth again. In the water, as during the night, you have seen nothing. In coming forth you have found yourself in the brightness of day. At the same time you died and were born,

[1]C. K. Barrett, The Gospel according to St. John, SPCK, 1955, p. 70f.
[2]Catechetical Lectures, 20.4 (PG 33, 1079), op. cit. p. 264. See also

and this wholesome water has become for you both a tomb and a mother.[2]

And the poetic Ephraim the Syrian (306–373) wrote:

O womb! which daily brings forth without pain the sons of the kingdom of heaven. They descend indeed with their faults and their stains, but they rise as pure infants. For baptism becomes a second womb for them, which in bringing them forth makes young men out of old, as the river Jordan restored Naaman to his youth.[3]

A baptismal inscription of the fifth century says:

Here a people of godly race are born for heaven; the Spirit gives them life in the fertile waters. The Church-Mother, in these waves, bears her children like virginal fruit she has conceived by the Holy Spirit.[4]

The linking of images in these is interesting. Baptism is thought of as the water of both death and life. It is described as a 'second womb', transforming those who are brought forth from it, as Naaman was, of whom II Kings says "his flesh was restored like the flesh of a little child". (5: 12). The church is in baptism called a 'mother' from whom her children are born by a virgin birth.[5]

Here then is another fundamental baptismal image, linked

Ambrose, *De Sacramentis*, 3.1 (PL 16, 450), and Theodore, *Baptismal Homilies*, 3.10

[3]The reference is to II Kings 4: 1–14. The word in the LXX for 'wash' in vv. 10 and 13 is *baptizein*.

[4]Inscription of Sextus III, 432–440, Schuster, *Liber Sacramentorum*, vol. I p. 32, quoted in Lucien Deiss, *Early Service of the Liturgy*, Alba House, 1963, p. 197.

[5]There is a school of obstetrics which encourages mothers to give birth

theologically and biblically to that of dying and rising, so that this too is passing 'through the waters'. Birth is not then an alternative image to death and deliverance, for it comes to us (in John 3, Romans 8, etc.) in the context of the coming, dying, and rising of Christ. Birth and death are not set over against one another as optional ways of looking at baptism or salvation. Birth and death are bound together, as the mystery – Paul would say the 'offence' – at the heart of the Christian faith. We cannot detach the image of birth and construct a new theology of baptism upon it, but (not least because it is so universal and everyday) it sheds added light on the mystery and reveals fresh meaning in baptism as the witness to it.

The image of birth highlights a feature of baptism which we have noticed already. Birth happens to us. We do not ask, or offer, to be born; we do not even submit to being born. Birth precedes all will, all choosing, all thinking. Birth is a paradigm of helplessness. When we ask then why baptism is like birth we realise it is because baptism is the sacrament of helplessness, passivity, dependence.

> Baptism is something that *happens* to the man at the Church's hand . . . The baptismal act in which he enters the Church, like the birth whereby he enters the world, is something done rather on him than by him . . . Even when the submission to Baptism is the believer's own act, this is so.[6]

Baptism is in fact the celebration of our helplessness, our dependence upon God. Until we are born 'over again', 'from above', born through water and the Spirit, we cannot

in a shallow pool, in the belief that water is the most reassuring environment for the newborn to enter.

[6] P. T. Forsyth, *The Church and the Sacraments*, Longmans, Green & Co., 1917, p. 194.

understand nor feel at home in the kingdom of God; we cannot enter, we cannot begin. This may be deeply objectionable to us: not dedication nor piety, not my repentance nor even my faith, brings me to this. Being born was not something I gave or did: the capacity to give or undertake only then began to grow within me. Nor does it grow without difficulty. The impulse to give is matched – time and again outmatched – by the impulse, every bit as strong, to clutch and keep. Without that instinct of course I would not have survived, but gradually I come to sense that it is possible to hold on without clutching, and that she whom I so anxiously (and sometimes angrily) seize hold of will not stop loving and attending to me if we are for a time separated, or if it seems so to me. She is the giver. She has given herself to me, and in doing that she has given me myself.

So it is between us and God. The birth of this relationship is not a gift we offer him, though it can feel as if it is. It is not 'dedication'. It is rather the reverse: it is God's commitment to us, each one, that is the root of it all. Only within that can we begin to understand about giving, how it feels to give; only now can we start to discover what we have that can be given, and shared, and even lavishly squandered. The meeting between Jesus and the unnamed woman at Simon's house describes the clumsy, gauche impulsiveness of the relationship between the not long born and the Lord (Mark 14: 3–9). But however tidy, appropriate, or practised she, or any of us, might become in our Christian lives, and whatever else, more suitable maybe, she or any of us might have to offer, there would never be a better gift, nor ever better given, than that. It is like the baby, grabbing the beginning-to-be-loved one. Only by seizing can giving develop. We may resent the fact that it is like this, but there is nothing for it but to accept that it is so. It is that kind of relationship that baptism initiates, all one way at first, but gradually expanding into insight, imagination, generosity and love.

The image of birth holds more. The love of mother for child has to take quite practical form – the tedium and burden of the long months of preparing for birth; the feeding, washing, soothing; the anxiety and exhaustion. But that is not what her love is. These are vivid signs of it, but her love is behind and beneath all that, deep and strong enough (and deepening and strengthening as the days go by) to deal with the sheer demanding selfishness, the egocentricity, of her child, until at last she sees the first signs of recognition, delight, and love. And this happens because she loved first. Sometimes it looks as if our relationship to God is nothing more than an endless cycle of sinning, confession, and forgiveness. Sometimes that is how the love of God is preached and taught. But we are not loved because we are sinners; it is not our sin that evokes his love. The love of God is not even as conditional as that. If his love were essentially forgiveness, then we could never be sure that we still mattered, once forgiven; we would always be tempted to sin to be sure that he still loved us. It would be his wrath, not his love, that we secretly needed. The passage to new life that baptism proclaims is like this. Growing into the new life is full of problems, anxiety and vexation, and our attempts at it, even our most sophisticated attempts, can be very clumsy. But the immense freedom we are given is still not modified or taken away from us.

That is how unconditional grace is, and it is to that unconditionality that baptism points. Grace comes first, it is prior – 'prevenient' is a favourite traditional description of it. Faith and love grow from what God has done once and for all in Christ. They follow upon baptism; they are

73

consequences of it rather than preconditions. God initiates, we respond – not the other way round. We know this because it is like being born (I John 4: 17–19).[7]

This way of looking at baptism is closely related to what we find in the New Testament concerning children, their place in the kingdom, and the meaning of this for all would-be disciples. Eduard Schweizer, commenting on Matthew 18: 1–5, says:

> The metaphor of becoming a child . . . in time came to be associated with baptism, as similarly in I Peter 2: 1ff, and was interpreted in the community in the light of their doctrine of baptism as referring to birth through water and the Spirit.[8]

and on Mark 10: 13–15:

> Jesus becomes angry with (the disciples) . . . It would appear that his reply defends the children, who are passive, and not the adults who are bringing the children . . . This much is clear: the children play no active role and cannot defend themselves against the overzealous disciples. But this is the reason they are blessed – just because they have nothing to show for themselves. They cannot count on any achievements of their own – their hands are empty like those of a beggar . . . God's kingdom is promised to man without his desiring it.[9]

Ernest Best discussing these and similar passages writes:

[7]See O. Cullman, *Baptism in the New Testament*, SCM, 1950, p. 20: "It belongs to the essence of this general Baptism effected by Jesus, that it is offered in entire independence of the decision of faith and understanding of those who benefit from it. Baptismal grace has its foundation here, and it is in the strictest sense 'prevenient grace'". See also P. T. Forsyth p. 195.

[8]*The Good News according to Matthew*, SPCK, 1976, p.361.

[9]*The Good News according to Mark*, SPCK, 1970, p.206f.

The Kingdom is to be received as children receive. But how does a child receive? Commentators have written variously of the innocence, simplicity, ingenuousness, receptiveness of children. All such interpretations, apart from the last, tend to romanticise the child in a way foreign to the ancient world. . . . A child trusts adults; he has confidence in them; he receives from them what they offer. So the disciple is to trust God and receive the kingdom.[10]

We might call this 'the logic of baptism'. It is a logic which gets behind conventional piety, to the point where our relationship to God is like that of new born babe to mother. I am in Christ simply baptismally, not even 'by faith alone' but 'by baptism alone'. Baptism is the paradigm of helplessness – and so of grace at work. Confession of faith, repentance and forgiveness, dedication of life, will all, and again and again, mark the unfolding life of the Christian, but the Christian will never be more in Christ than at baptism. What follows is not the 'completion' of baptism as it is sometimes miscalled – for our baptism must be complete in itself if The Baptism which it proclaims is complete in itself once for all – but the discovery and the appropriation of baptism as the underlying structure of the Christian life.

This has important implications for the controversy about infant and believers' baptism. We are not entitled, I believe, to adopt a dogmatic position and say magisterially 'paedobaptism is wrong', or 'believers' baptism is wrong'. What could 'wrong' mean in such a context? – heretical? theologically questionable? of no effect? not baptism at all? Simply to attack one or other view is arrogance, and anything but 'orthodox' – 'rightly glorifying'. What we can do, indeed must do, is to press the logic we see in baptism, and follow the direction which that logic takes.

[10]*Disciples and Discipleship*, T. & T. Clark, 1986, p. 96.

We must be clear that the important distinction is not between the baptizing of adults and the baptizing of infants, but between the baptizing of believers and the baptizing of infants who are not yet believers. There is no reason why baptism as receiving, as deliverance, as birth, should not be appropriate for adults. Adults need to discover this if they are to understand and accept God's gracious love for them. But it would seem by this logic that it is also right to baptize infants, who in every other sense are dependent on the love, power, and wisdom of others.

Can we however say any more than that? History does not resolve the controversy. It is necessary to bear in mind that what we see of the life and practice of the church in the New Testament is development, not finality. Some features quite quickly took on the form which has remained substantially the same ever since. The direction of the Christian mission out from Jerusalem, from the home base, to the Gentiles, and the wider world is one; and the eucharist is probably another. But other elements remained fluid well beyond the New Testament period. The role of women in the church is one example, and church order another. Baptism belongs to this second category. For a long time beyond the primitive church the practice of baptism remained fluid as new situations challenged and modified existing thinking.[11]

The first to be baptized were of course adults, upon

[11] See Forsyth, op. cit. p. 204: "The full scope of baptism, or any other institution or doctrine, could not be reached in the practice of the first century. Let us correct any magic by a scriptural principle to which both Protestant forms bear witness. Both can express the evangelical conception of faith. And in both Baptism acts on the subject psychologically and not subliminally, in the one case by a crisis and the other by a nurture. In the one case it embodies a new and fontal experience, in the other it begins a regenerative education, or what would now be called a creative evolution". On this basis he goes on to commend the use of both practices.

repentance and faith. There is evidence to suggest that children were, at least sometimes, baptized along with their parents, but this was probably not because they were children but because they were part of the household. (Acts 16: 15, 33; 18: 8; I Corinithians 1: 16). The argument for paedobaptism must begin as cautiously as that.

> It was thought fitting to receive children into the fellowship of Christ and the Church, but no special rite of infant baptism was ever devised. In the early days the baptism of children was something almost 'incidental', a sort of appendage to the baptism of adults, which was always the main concern.[12]

Adult baptism was the norm (though the first Christians would not have dreamed of putting it like that). The Faith and Order Report *Baptism, Eucharist and Ministry* simply states,

> While the possibility that infant baptism was also practised in the apostolic age cannot be excluded, baptism upon personal profession of faith is the most clearly attested pattern in the New Testament.[13]

R. W. Jenson writes,

> The history of baptism since ca. AD 500 can be told as the history of ancient baptism's disintegration ... The universalized practice of infant baptism was the main disintegrating force. Manifestly, the initiation (just described) was designed primarily for adults – in a straightforward response to the New Testament mandate, which concerned, after all, a rite of repentance. Yet the church had also baptized

---

[12]Burkhard Neunheuser, "Baptism", *Sacramentum Mundi*, Burns & Oates 1968, vol. I, p. 139.
[13]*Faith and Order Paper No. 111*, World Council of Churches, 1982, "Baptism", para. 11.

infants as far back as our sources allow sure conclusions. Until the fifth century, that 'also' was the key factor.[14]

Like other elements in the life of the early church, however, baptism was marked by the conviction that the Parousia was imminent. They had no plans for a second generation church. Obedience here and now was what mattered, and not prudent policy-making for the future.[15] When it did begin to become clear that it was not going to be quite as they had at first imagined some rethinking was necessary, but it was a long time before the age of baptism was a matter of considered regulation, let alone of theology. In practice both adults and infants were baptized. At length, as we have seen, an emergent doctrine of original sin, coupled with a strong emphasis on the cleansing significance of baptism, led to a 'doctrine', a theology, of infant baptism. By the end of the fifth century paedobaptism was the universal norm. However, if paedobaptists insist that merely because believers' baptism was the norm in the early period that does not make it the norm for us, they must by the same argument allow that merely because later on infant baptism became the norm does not make it right for the church since. The argument from history is a two-edged sword.

It is important then to distinguish between what the church has in practice done – the argument from history – and what the church believes, now as well as then – the argument from theology. These are not of course necessarily separate or unrelated, but they are distinct:

> We may look to the New Testament for a law commanding infant baptism: we may look to the Church of the Apostolic Age for precedents to justify the practice: and we shall look

[14]op. cit. p. 159f.
[15]Jenson, op. cit. p. 160.

in vain. Infant baptism, if it is to be vindicated at all, must be vindicated on other grounds; and those grounds must be of two kinds, theological and pastoral. We must be satisfied that the practice really accords with our best understanding of the nature of the Divine grace that is at work in the salvation of men; and we must be satisfied that the practice meets a real human need, which cannot be met adequately in other ways.[16]

Some scholars, Cullmann and Jeremias for example, seek to show that infant baptism did in fact take place in the early church.[17] But Aland, though a paedobaptist by conviction, rejects any attempt to prove by research that it did.[18] Karl Barth, in *The Teaching of the Church Regarding Baptism*, expounds theologically what he considers to be the biblical doctrine of baptism, dismissing the 'household baptism' argument of some paedobaptists in one withering paragraph, and expounding, from *within* the classic tradition which has always held to infant baptism, the theological case for believers' baptism as the norm.[19]

Theological reasons have to be sought either for paedobaptism *in spite of the early practice*, or for believers' baptism *in spite of the change of practice* after 500 AD:

> . . . the question now runs: is the New Testament practice of believers' baptism a temporary phenomenon arising out of the 'special missionary situation' of the church? Or does believers' baptism rather enshrine an essential truth of the Gospel which is belied by the administration of baptism to infants?

[16]See T. W. Manson, *The Church's Ministry*, Hodder & Stoughton, 1948, p. 87.

[17]Cullmann, op. cit. J. Jeremias, *Infant Baptism in the First Four Centuries*, SCM, 1960.

[18]*Did the Early Church Baptize Infants?*, SCM, 1963.

[19]ET SCM, 1948, p. 44f.

The Baptist cannot now simply say: infant baptism is not recorded in the New Testament, *therefore* it is wrong. Rather he must show that the baptism only of believers arises out of the Gospel itself.[20]

The issue is made even more complicated by the fact that even when paedobaptism became the norm, the church continued to use, with little modification, a rite based on believers' baptism. This was made to work by means of god-parents, who in effect represented the mind and will of the child and spoke for the child, so that he or she could be treated as if an adult:

> ... through the intermediary of their god-parents infants are treated at their baptism as if they were adults: they renounce Satan, confess the faith, and state that they wish to be baptized.[21]

Reformed churches have tended to stop short of a thoroughgoing and distinctive infant baptism rite. Expressions like "this promise is for believers *and also* for their children", or "little children do not understand these things *yet the promise is also to them*" (Jenson's 'also' actually set in the liturgy!) betray a worrying theological unsteadiness. The implication is that baptism is 'also' for children, not in their own right but because of their parents' faith and membership – rather as they are included in the family passport, able to travel only when and where their parents travel. This is at bottom the argument for infant baptism from 'covenant theology'. The claim is that a child qualifies for baptism through the parents' membership of the covenant people. It is not clear however,

[20]Geoffrey Wainwright, *Christian Initiation*, p. 48f. This is what Barth did show and what Wainwright proceeds to show first here and later more fully in his *Doxology*, 1980.
[21]*Sacramentum Mundi* I, p. 139.

that the New Testament teaching on baptism seeks to base it on the idea of the Old Testament covenant relationship between God and his people Israel. On the contrary, baptism appears as a rite that is quite new, unencumbered by Jewish significance: indeed it is contrasted with circumcision, which was the sign of initiation into covenant membership. Baptism, not circumcision, is the sign of incorporation into Christ, and that is true for Gentiles and Jews alike (Acts 8: 26–40, 10: 24–48, 11: 1–18; Romans 2, 3; Galatians 2, 3, 4, 5: 1–12; Ephesians 2: 11–22). What is more, at the heart of baptism is the individual's relationship to God in Christ in her or his own right, rather than in any sense derivatively. If that is true for an adult, must it not also be true for a child, for is there not but one baptism?

There are three possible positions. The first is a doctrine of believers' baptism, the unambiguous teaching and practice of the Baptist churches. The second is a thoroughgoing doctrine of infant baptism, with a place for adult baptism where need be, but with a more or less single rite based on infant baptism. The third position, widespread among the churches, favours infant baptism as the normal rite of initiation into the church, but also provides for believers' baptism for adults, that is, baptism upon repentance and faith. This third position looks sensible, and is undoubtedly well intentioned, but it is in fact an attempt to have it both ways. It is to hold two doctrines of baptism instead of one – a paedobaptism theology for infants, and a believers' baptism theology in the case of adults – two positions purporting to be one, and effectively neutralising each other. Small wonder, then, that church members find it hard to grasp the meaning of baptism.

Some union churches – the United Reformed Church in the U. K. for instance – have judged either that the doctrine of baptism is not a salient ecumenical issue, or else that it should allow a reconciled coexistence, and embrace both traditions and practices within one fellowship. This no doubt means that the former baptist members of the united church, the Disciples of Christ, can continue in these congregations to practise believers' baptism, the rite for which is incorporated in the official Book of Services.[22] But is there a distinction intended between that rite and the meaning behind it, and the baptism of an adult entrant in a formerly paedobaptist congregation? And what happens when, quite properly as time goes by, congregations begin to feel less self-conscious about their pre-union traditions, and are joined by members from other traditions?

The Faith and Order Report No. 111 – *Baptism, Eucharist and Ministry* – suggests dual practice as a worthwhile ecumenical solution, but there is little in the report on Baptism as a whole to suggest that that arrangement would pose substantial difficulty. The lack of focus in this report does regrettably detract from its theological and radical ecumenical value; important issues are fudged.

Can we have it both ways? Barth says No, and opts for believers' baptism.[23] Geoffrey Wainwright too writes with candour and cogency of his theological move:

> I judge it to be a false dilemma which opposes K. Barth, with his view of baptism as a purely human act of confession (and therefore to be performed only in the case of believing subjects), and a Lutheran such as E. Schlink, with his view of baptism as a purely divine act upon a passive recipient (and therefore most suitably administered to infants). Rather is baptism the sacramental focus of both divine graciousness and the active human reception of God's gift: baptism is most fully itself when received upon profession of faith. This is a view to which I, stemming from a paedobaptist tradition

[22]*A Book of Services*, The Saint Andrew Press, 1980, "Baptism of Believers and Confirmation", pp. 50ff.
[23]op. cit. pp. 40ff.

82

(Methodist) came in writing my *Christian Initiation* (Lutterworth, 1969) and which I have expressed less hesitantly in subsequent articles. I now hold to the general preferability of baptism upon profession of faith and consider that it is infant baptism which needs justification as an exception which may, in a pluralist practice, enshrine certain values.[24]

That same rigour has to be used by those who want to expound a doctrine of infant baptism. If what I have called the 'logic of baptism' is followed through we find ourselves not merely with a case for infant baptism but with a radical doctrine of baptism and of the baptismal structures of the Christian life which can apply with equal integrity and validity to infants and adults. We must avoid the temptation to qualify the fullness of what is given in baptism, either by pointing away from it to a later and mature 'completion' of infant baptism, or by insisting upon a prior repentance and confession of faith as the condition for adult baptism. Of course the 'credo', the 'I believe', is important – but not *here*, not at *baptism*. Here the credo is that of the church. Into that the newcomer is received; within that the newcomer, child or adult, is held. This can be expressed vividly and convincingly in the liturgy of baptism itself (see Appendix).

As often as not, however, the problem about baptism for the individual and for the church arises not in theological but in pastoral terms. It is presented in the young adult who discovers the reality of the love of God and the Lordship of Christ in her or his life with such sweeping force that it is like a rebirth of identity and personality, and who wants a second baptism to match the second birth. It is presented in parents who hesitate to have their child baptized for fear of making a decision on behalf of their child which is not theirs to make, but which ought instead to be left for her or him to

[24]Geoffrey Wainwright, *Expository Times*, vol. 88, No. 5, p. 136.

make later, when able to understand and believe in a mature and adult fashion. These, frequently painful, pastoral needs the church must attend to.

Baptism is like birth: indeed it is a birth, a beginning. Beginnings are unrepeatable: we cannot get back behind them. Yet though we know that we cannot be born all over again, some may feel, by some deep perception in our being, that we had a bad start in life. There are grounds for believing that peri-natal or even pre-natal experience does lodge somewhere in our sub-memory. A welcoming womb, a sense of being wanted and cherished might be expected to leave me with an unaccountable yet undeniable sense of well-being ever after. But it could be very different. It could be a tense, anxious womb, as if she were not ready in herself for me, as if she were afraid of me and of what I might require of her, of the pain I might bring her. Or what if I were resented, a mistake, or a guilty secret kept until there was no way of keeping it any longer; or what if because of the bad feelings I set going in her I were simply feared and hated for being here? How could she keep all that from me, flesh of her flesh? Even if there is no such foetal memory, capable of being tapped and articulated in later life, it is all too true that because there is much more to birth than being physically delivered there are those who have had a bad start in life. There are those who are merely born, but not then enfolded in the loving, tending, and nourishing that a baby must have in order to grow resilient and secure. What can such a person then do? It is impossible to go back and be born again: birth is irreversible and no alternative life is available but this. Yet there is a way. What such a person can do is to work back through the bad and frightened feelings and revisit the past, even the deeply buried past, with skilled and sensitive help, and so be reconciled and put right, with self and others.

In very much the same way, there are those who were

merely baptized, but who did not then get the loving and the feeding necessary to grow and to mature, spiritually and emotionally. Yet such people can have a new start, with God, with self, and with others. The new start is not made by cancelling out the past: that cannot be done. There is no other life; there are already too many givens. The new start can be made by accepting the past for what it was, and for what it was not, and experiencing now, within a skilled and reassuring pastoral care, the acceptance, the warmth, the love, that seemed lacking before – and discovering that though it was not or could not be recognised it was always there, from the beginning, because it is nothing other than the love of God. We must not mistake what this means and what is taking place: it is nurturing, not baptism, that has been missing; and it is nurturing, not a rebaptism, that transforms and restores. Baptism, like birth, is only the beginning of growth. To resolve a sense of unreality about one's infant baptism, however painful that unreality may feel, by under-going another baptism, is merely a regression, a frightened denial of the present which in itself resolves nothing.

In their dealings with the issue of rebaptism the churches have sometimes seemed more anxious for orthodoxy than for loving understanding. A doctrinal answer to the problem, however correct, is of little pastoral use. Much more attention needs to be paid in these days to the cry for a new baptism. We must try to understand the lack of confidence some have in their baptism – was it real? is it enough? why can I not undergo it now, now that I believe and understand, now that I know I want it? We need to create effective pastoral relationships with those who feel unbaptized, within which the doubts and longings can be listened to and understood, and within which what we say makes sense and speaks to the needs they feel.

Blame must lie with irresponsible sermons which sow seeds

of that doubt and longing in the minds of those who want to explore the life of faith, and which speak to people as if they had not really been baptized at all, as if now, the moment of faith and commitment, is the moment of true birth and beginning. Some blame must lie with parents who have failed to fulfil what they undertook at their children's baptism to do for them. Some blame must lie with the church for forgetting about the baptism of its children, never referring to it, never telling them of it. If it has apparently meant nothing more to the church than an entry in a register, why should we suppose it will mean more to the infant once grown up? We may therefore need to look hard at what we effectively say and teach about baptism in the worship and nurture of the children of the church. We may also need to devise, with the help of those who feel unbaptized, a renewal of baptism that does justice both to their own infant baptism and to their newfound realisation of what the gospel of Christ crucified and risen means for them.

> When, after years, perhaps, of apathy or hostility to the Church and the Gospel, men and women who were baptized in infancy discover at last the love of Christ and are brought to faith and discipleship, what stronger proof could there be that the gracious word of God declared over them long ago was real and true and unrevoked, needing no repetition, but only glad recollection? Without their knowing it or perhaps even caring, God's sign of grace has in reality overarched the intervening years like the rainbow, his love pursuing them relentlessly until his claim upon their lives, once uttered, has in mercy and providence finally and joyfully been experienced, remembered, and acknowledged.[25]

Perhaps what I have described as analogous – baptism and

[25]Report of the Panel on Doctrine, *Church of Scotland General Assembly Reports*, 1983, p. 159.

birth – are in reality much more profoundly interrelated. Perhaps the intriguing and difficult conversation of John 3 means us to explore and discover in this an interrelatedness of great subtlety. It must be significant that both theologically and psychologically distress and despair are described specifically in terms of a lost child. R. S. Lee says "the difficulties which bring people to seek help are always matters of defective growth".[26] Elsewhere he speaks of the necessity, at times, of "living through one's broken infancy again". A psychotherapist describes pastoral work and therapy as "the reparenting of a lost child". The coincidences of perception and of imagery are too striking to be dismissed as mere analogy.[27]

There is another side to this. If we are to take the birth image in baptism seriously and not merely sentimentally, it follows also that we are making profound affirmations about God. Giving birth is the act of a woman, mother to the child who is born to her. How then shall we relate this to the faith which centres on God as Father?

The role of women and of femininity in the church and in

[26]*Principles of Pastoral Counselling*, SPCK, 1968, p. 27.

[27]Harry Guntrip describes this experience in therapy as follows: "The only cure for an ultimate sense of isolation and therefore meaninglessness in life, in anybody, is that someone should be able to get him back into a relationship that will give life some point again. Can we be sure the patient can stand its being uncovered, or dare we leave him alone with it lest it break out willy-nilly and destroy him? Can the patient be sure that we can stand it and support him until a new thrust and a new meaning in life begins to be born again in him? One cannot always know the answer to these questions, but where patient and therapist are prepared to stick it out together, then, at the risk of tragic failure, a profoundly rewarding success can, in my experience, in a significant number of cases be achieved. I do not know how this can be statistically validated by the hard pressed general practitioner of analytic therapy, but the patient knows when he is literally 'born again' ". *Psychoanalytic Theory, Therapy and the Self*, Maresfield Library, London, 1977, p. 195f.

Christian faith has always been a troubled one. We shall return to some practical aspects of this in the next chapter, but here we must recognise something of its effect on our understanding of God and of the Christian's relationship to God. Damage has been done to men and to women by the simplistic attribution of superiority – God-given superiority – to maleness within the church, and immense impoverishment has been caused to spirituality as well as to theology by the perverse and complacent failure of both men and women to explore what it means that the image of God is male and female (Gen. 1: 27). This is not, as is sometimes alleged, an unnecessary tinkering with the faith of the church, and with the sense of the Scriptures, in order to accommodate Christianity to new cultural fashions. The images of femininity and of motherliness in God are already there in Scripture: the poets and prophets of the Old Testament are more daring in their insights into the rich nature of God and of our relationship to God than their Christian successors have for the most part been (Numbers 11: 12; Deut. 32: 11; Psalm 22: 9, 131: 2; Isaiah 31: 5, 42: 14, 46: 3, 49: 15, 66: 12).

What has this to do with baptism? It is a baptism issue because baptism challenges the very male values by which we commonly (men and women) characterise spirituality and the life of faith. We value faith in terms of its strength, we admire the Christian who does not break down, who is untouched by doubt or uncertainty; we are impressed by the impassive, unshaken reaction to whatever comes. We announce at baptism that "He/she is now engaged to confess the faith of Christ crucified, and to be his faithful soldier and servant unto life's end": do little girls grow to be soldiers? do we even want all our little boys to be *that* kind of Christian disciple? What place can such a view of Christian spirituality have for weakness or indecision, or for tenderness and tears? Yet does not our salvation rest upon the vulnerability, the gentleness, the unaggressiveness, indeed the tears, of the Saviour? We allow, perhaps encourage, an understanding of faith in which it is the cerebral, the rational, what is 'understood' and 'thought', to dominate over what is felt and intuited. Yet the obstacles and attacks the Christian meets will often be difficult or threatening precisely because they assail us at a non-rational or infra-rational level of perception and response – because they defy logic, do not 'make sense'; because they have to do with the way we feel, with our sense of who we are, what we are doing, and where we are going. When that happens we need to be able to draw on resources of inner stability and serenity that have nothing to do with fighting back, or coming off best, but instead allow us to make mistakes without guilt, to lose a battle or an argument without shame, and so to be able to love our enemies. Harry Guntrip, who has done much to relate the life of faith to the search for meaning and wholeness, said that there is a taboo on tenderness in our culture; that the one great crime of twentieth century mankind is to be weak; and that it is becoming all too rare to acknowledge this. The spirituality to which all this points has hints sometimes of womanliness and motherliness, and sometimes of childlikeness and infancy. Naturally it will be so, for baptism speaks both of mothering and of being mothered.

A member of the community of Taize, speaking of what it is that brings young people there in such numbers year after year, said, "We need to go back and back to the sources of faith, and we need to be willing to begin again and again". The birth that is baptism is not a single beginning: it is the sign of a lifetime of beginnings.[28] Such beginnings may be major life-changing events, or they may be very quiet and private discoveries. They may come in joyfulness or in mourning, in

[28] See Lampe, op. cit. p. 45.

achievement or in breakdown. They will however always be characterised by a readiness to receive, and to admit our powerlessness, by an openness to the truth about ourselves and what we have yet to discover and become. They will not require us to write off the past, as if it were of no value to God or to us – simply that we be willing to move on. It is for such a life, such an attitude to living, that baptism prepares us.

Chapter Five

BELONGING

The three images of baptism which we have discussed – washing, deliverance, and birth – each in its own way witnesses to the unique identity of each person in Christ which baptism affirms. However many may arrive for baptism at the same service, they can only be baptized one at a time, and the deliberate announcement of each Christian name and the 'I baptize you . . .' for each one emphasises the fact that in this the church declares the individuality of each in Christ.

Yet because baptism is 'into Christ' that means it is entry into the community of those who are of Christ, the body of Christ, the church. With baptism comes belonging. This was the most dramatic characteristic of the early church, a radical and new kind of relatedness to one another, and it was the issue at the centre of the first great controversy the young church faced. Being a Jew meant belonging to the covenant community, and the sign of this was circumcision. There were those who therefore believed that entry into the new covenant community lay through the old, and so, it was argued, circumcision preceded baptism, for Gentiles as well as for Jews. Others however recognised how profoundly everything had changed. Baptism was not like circumcision. It was not simply a symbolic rite of initiation. It was 'in the name of Christ', and so they came to realise that it proclaimed a relationship to Christ so radical that it came to be described as being 'in Christ', and as baptism 'into Christ'. (Acts 2: 41–47, 4: 32–37, 10, 11; Romans 6: 3–4, 12: 4–5; I Cor. 11: 18–34, 12: 4–27; II Cor. 5: 16–19; Gal. 3: 23–29, 5: 2–12, 6: 12–16; Eph.2: 11–22, 3:5–12; Col. 1: 21–23, 2:8–14, 3: 1–17).

> If to be baptized is to be 'in Christ', to be 'in Christ' is to belong to the Church . . . Being in Christ, being in the church, being in the Spirit – these are but different ways of asserting the same one great reality.[1]

To be baptized then meant not merely a new identity for oneself, but also a new relationship to other members of the community of the baptized, including some whom society usually separated from others. Indeed the new identity did not merely lead to new relationships: the new identity each one discovered was found in and through membership of the new community. Baptism, the sacrament of dependence, points forward to a life that is not self-sufficient, that has indeed renounced self-sufficiency as a way of life and all attempts to go it alone, and instead has turned to others, to create with them the interdependence that is the mark of Christian maturity. To the first Christians this must have been both amazing and disturbing. To realise that as a Jew you could not belong in the church without sharing it with your Gentile fellow-Christians; or that when the church gathered at your house for worship and the breaking of bread, your servants, instead of looking after things, would sit down alongside you as if they were your best friends; or at the Supper, to find yourself sitting alongside women who in synagogue had always sat elsewhere . . . all this up-ending of what was understood and familiar must have been acutely difficult. And we may imagine, to look at it from the other end, how it must have felt to be a slave, or a woman, in the church. The roles, and the sense of 'place' known instinctively from a lifetime's habit, were set aside, and something quite new took their place. All this was, and is, the result of baptism.

[1]Neville Clark, *An Approach to the Theology of the Sacraments*, SCM. 1956, p. 24f.

There are no doubt modern parallels of this daunting belonging into which we are drawn in membership in the church, but to what – or to whom – in broader terms do Christians belong? To what, or to whom, does baptism into Christ commit us?

In the first place baptism unites us to the church past. John Croall, who founded the Croall Lectureship, was a member of St. Cuthbert's Church in Edinburgh in the first half of the last century. When in the 1880s the interior of St. Cuthbert's was reconstructed, John Croall's son Robert gave the new pulpit in memory of his father. The base of the pulpit is the foundation-stone of the present church, and it in turn rests on a deeper base made from stones from the pre-Reformation church that earlier stood on that site. We cannot found a new church, nor found the church over again. We never really build a church from scratch. We are to build on what is already there, the legacy of the past. And we can only build because there is that already there. In baptism we are brought into fellowship with the church that has been here before us, owning what sometimes seems strange and remote, even what was sin and failure, but joyfully entering into the chain of sacrament, witness and worship in our own time and place. When a font is carved from Iona marble, or from a rock taken from the hillside above Bethlehem as in Coventry Cathedral, the symbolism is clear and correct. Baptism unites us in solidarity with the church past.

Moreover, baptism is the sacrament of our ecumenicity, of solidarity with the church present. Geoffrey Wainwright cites passages in the Epistles in which he claims baptism appears "as a ritual sign of Christian unity".[2] The conviction that there is 'one baptism' prevents any privatising or denominationalising of the sacrament. The majority of churches accept one

[2] *Doxology*, p. 126.

another's baptism. Although deeply divided doctrinally, and divided in practical terms at the communion table, they can agree that baptism by water in the Trinitarian name is authentic, and does not require provisional baptism or rebaptism. In the United Kingdom, for example, a common certificate of baptism has been issued which gives the names of the agreeing churches, all of which practise infant baptism as the rule.

The Second Vatican Council Decree on Ecumenism says, "All who have been justified by faith in baptism are incorporated into Christ; they therefore have a right to be called Christians, and with good reason are accepted as brothers by the children of the Catholic Church".[3] "Baptism is then the sacramental bond of unity, indeed the foundation of communion among all Christians"[4] Does this however mean more than the acceptance of the baptism of an individual, irrespective of who or which church was the baptizer? Does it carry with it sacramental recognition of another church? Perhaps not yet: since the times of the heretic Donatists and Montanists baptism has been seen as containing its validity within itself, no matter who administers it, or at least as a rite so limited on its own that the proper completion of it in episcopal confirmation will eventually take care of anything lacking in the water baptism of infancy. Yet if baptism is seen to be the sacrament of incorporation into the church, even this limited degree of ecumenical accord is important — at least as important as eucharistic fellowship would be. It has a knock-on significance which must call in

---

[3]*Decree on Ecumenism*, 3, Vatican II, *Unitate redintegratio*, 21 November 1964, *Vatican Council II, The Conciliar and Post Conciliar Documents*, ed. Austin Flannery, Scholarly Resources Inc., 1975, p. 455f.

[4]*Directory Concerning Ecumenical Matters*, I. 11, S.P.U.C, *Ad Totam Ecclesiam*, 14 May 1967, op. cit. p. 487.

question other attempts to distance one church from another. That means however that the potential for further ecumenical progress will depend on the seriousness with which baptism is regarded as the sacrament of incorporation and belonging together in Christ.

Member churches in the Faith and Order Commission of the World Council of Churches have shown something of that seriousness in the publication of the now famous Paper No. 111, *Baptism, Eucharist and Ministry*.[5]

These issues were on the agenda of the first Faith and Order Conference in 1927, so church leaders can scarcely be accused of being over hasty, but though it has taken a long time to arrive at an agreed statement the importance of this milestone should not be underrated – not least because it now counts among its signatories a much wider cross-section of the world church, nationally as well as denominationally, than could have been imagined in 1927. Hans-George Link, a member of the Faith and Order Commission, wrote soon afterwards

> how, after the *unanimous* vote in favour of the text, the worthy members of our commission leapt up from their seats to long sustained applause, much embracing and the offering of a fervent prayer of thanksgiving by our moderator, Prof. Missiotis of Athens. Everyone present must have felt that they were witnessing a historic moment in the history of the ecumenical movement. It can in fact be said that on 12 January 1982 a fifty-five year long ecumenical journey reached its – provisional – destination . . .[6]

Of course BEM is an achievement, yet many when they came to read the eagerly awaited text found it disappointing.

[5] World Council of Churches, 1982.
[6] World Council of Churches "Letter on Evangelism", April 1983.

There are indications that earlier drafts (the Accra 'agreed statement' of 1974, for example) have had to be greatly modified for official publication to be acceptable.[7] Compelled to be a diplomatic statement, it fails to face fundamental differences on baptism, particularly the important divide between the paedobaptist and believers' baptist positions, and the continuing covert adult baptism norm that has persisted in officially paedobaptist churches. It may be, however, that from even such a narrow common ground the churches may find themselves able to engage less defensively in a robust conversation in which individual traditions can be clearly explained and sympathetically listened to. Certainly as long as churches feel themselves permitted privately to think what they like about the relation of the baptized to the church, and to interpret 'church' in their own way, the value of an agreed statement is greatly limited and the concept of a common baptism largely romantic.[8]

A commentator on the story of this ecumenical debate says, "agreement on the theology of baptism (has) proved relatively easy only because baptism (has) been isolated from its contexts".[9] If the reality of a common baptism is seriously faced it will eventually burst open our closely guarded eucharists and structures of ministry, for ultimately neither eucharist nor ministry can be properly described except in terms of baptism. One baptism leads to one ministry in Christ, and to one table in Christ. As one of the church responses to BEM puts it: "We must beware of shouting 'baptismal unity, baptismal unity' where honestly there is no

[7]See Gunter Wagner and Lewis S. Mudge, *Ecumenical Perspectives on Baptism, Eucharist and Ministry*, ed. Max Thurian, World Council of Churches, 1983, pp. 12–45 and Appendix i, pp. 209–214.

[8]A searching discussion of this is to be found in Geoffrey Wainwright, *Doxology*, pp. 308–314.

[9]Ernst Lange, quoted in *Ecumenical Perspectives*, p. 44.

more than a common use of words and language".[10] A delegate from the U.S. Disciples of Christ is reported as describing BEM as a "miracle – the most radical thing the World Council has ever done" because of its implications for church reunion,[11] but just how genuinely radical it is remains to be seen.

Christians are called to seek more than a theological consensus on a common baptism: they are summoned by the Gospel to express a genuine baptismal solidarity with one another, and to follow in obedience the unfolding relationships to which that solidarity leads.

> Baptism . . . prevents the separation of faith from community . . . Into the Kingdom proclaimed by any recognisable version of the gospel . . . we enter together or not at all . . . The one whose hope is founded in baptism cannot have salvation by himself.[12]

Common baptism then calls in question the fragmentation of the church, for in declaring 'one baptism' a stubbornly divided church – divided for instance at the Table – contradicts itself. But the one baptism in which all share on equal terms has implications for other sets of relationships within the church, those for instance between men and women, and between adult and child.

The breaking down of barriers in the young church between women and men, as well as between Gentile and Jew, and slave and master, has already been referred to. The new relationships cannot have been easy. Those who had been Jews had grown up with a clear tradition of the proper

[10]*Ecumenical Perspectives*, p. 18; see also pp. 213ff.
[11]Quoted in the WCC Ecumenical Press Service release, January 16, 1982.
[12]Jenson, op. cit. pp. 147, 150.

roles for men and women in synagogue and in daily life, and for the growing numbers of Gentile Christians too the contrast between what happened in church and what happened elsewhere must have been every bit as hard to come to terms with.

Centuries on, this is still a problem for the church, though in some respects the tables are now turned, and it is the world which challenges the church to change. When the history of this comes to be written it will tell of an astonishing mixture of progress and reaction in the church, and of the paradox that the very movement which first called in question the relegation of women to a subordinate status came to structure and to rationalise, in its own life and thought, a new subservience which is only now being seriously called in question.

The focus of the question has become the theology and practice of ministry, and whether women are permitted to exercise ministry and authority in the church on the same basis as men. This is a matter of burning controversy for the Anglican Communion, and in some degree for the Roman Catholic Church also. Yet even in some Reformed churches which have officially resolved the question, and certainly in the Church of Scotland, which admitted women to the eldership in 1966 and to the ministry in 1968, the controversy goes on. The difficulty of achieving any kind of consensus between or within churches is aptly illustrated in the well-meaning but undeniably fence-sitting position adopted by the World Council of Churches Faith and Order Commission in its Report *Baptism, Eucharist and Ministry*:

> Both women and men must discover together their contributions to the service of Christ in the Church. The Church must discover the ministry which can be provided by women as well as that which can be provided by men. A

deeper understanding of the comprehensiveness of ministry which reflects the interdependence of men and women needs to be more widely manifested in the life of the Church.

Though they agree on this need, the churches draw different conclusions as to the admission of women to the ordained ministry. An increasing number of churches have decided that there is no biblical or theological reason against ordaining women, and many of them have subsequently proceeded to do so. Yet many churches hold that the tradition of the Church in this regard must not be changed.[13]

Both Scripture and tradition are summoned in support of the view of those who would limit the vocation of women in the church. At the core of that limitation is the conviction, deeply and conscientiously felt, that whatever peripheral ministries may be allowed to women a sacramental ministry is exclusively and specifically for men. The one who breaks bread and raises the cup re-enacts what Jesus did, represents Jesus, and does so in the succession of those to whom the Lord delivered the apostolic ministry. The ministry was given by a man to men. That, it is argued, is not a historical accident, nor even merely a matter of culture. It has its source in the very nature of the Godhead, and it is determinative for all time.[14]

There are a number of ways of calling this theology in question, but fundamental to these is the significance of baptism. Behind all Christian life and vocation, behind the church's ministry and apostleship, lies baptism. This is the figure by which Jesus chose to describe his own ministry as the one sent. It began for him in a baptismal event; it

[13]Para. 18.
[14]See e.g. H. M. Conn, "Feminist Theology", *New Dictionary of Theology*, IVP, 1988, pp. 255ff.

culminated in that going through the waters of suffering, alienation, and death which he called his 'baptism'. Life and obedience for Jesus was ministry, and the sign of ministry was baptism. That, simply, is the significance of baptism. It is incorporation into life in Christ, into the ministry of Christ. It is in baptism that the Christian's living, worshipping, and serving is grounded. As Jesus regarded his utter self-giving as his 'baptism', so for the Christian there is no more to be given than that which baptism calls for – nothing less than her or his utter self-giving in Christ to the Father through the Spirit. There is fundamentally only one ministry, for all ministry stems from Jesus' ministry. Since baptism also, because of its singleness, affirms the breaking down of human divisions, so that there is 'neither male nor female', then by baptism there can be no fragmenting of the one ministry, as between men and women (or for that matter between Jew and Gentile). Any such division or separation, any excluding of either, limits and calls in question the baptism of those who are so excluded: it alleges that they are less than wholly in Christ. Indeed, it also limits and questions the baptism of those whose ministry is preferred, for it too becomes a fragment only of the one baptism. Exclusion and separation of ministry denies the integrity of baptism, that very quality which is the baptismal gift of Christ to the church. Such is the logic of baptism: the ministry of women and men is unconditionally equivalent.

This of course does not rule out all distinctiveness of ministry. In order to use and deploy the gifts of the Spirit to the community, the church may call and direct individuals to particular tasks. All Christians ought to be enabled to discern their vocation, instead of distinguishing between those who 'have a vocation' (or worse, 'go into the church'), and those who, by implication, have none. But distinctiveness of ministry is between one baptized individual and another;

the logic of baptism does not allow for discrimination based on sex, any more than on race or colour. To exclude women, because they are women, from ministry of any sort is to repudiate their baptism, for it is at their baptism that their acceptability and their individuality in Christ is unconditionally claimed and celebrated. The question of women ministers or priests is decisively answered at the font. Those who would disallow the sacramental ministry of women must answer the question about their baptism. In the Faith and Order Commission's report, the theology of baptism in the first section should have left no room for equivocation about the role of women in the last section.[15]

Children too are often marginalised in the church, and a human instead of a Christian distinction between adult and child persists which the rigorous evangelical logic of baptism must be allowed to challenge. Historically, the Supper was reached through the often lengthy pre-baptism catechumenate, and was the immediate and joyful reward of adult baptism. It was clear to everyone that baptism was the precondition of receiving communion – so clear that presumably nothing else had to be said about admission to the Supper; that is what baptism was.[16] The shift from adult to infant baptism as the norm however had the effect of splitting the rite into two distinct elements, one (water baptism) proclaiming remission of sins, and a second much later, proclaiming the gift of the Spirit. This distinction originally arose as a matter of practice and order; water baptism was delegated to the local presbyter, but the giving of the Spirit by anointing and laying on hands remained the prerogative of the bishop who was the guardian of order. As the period between these lengthened, they became separate

[15]Compare "Baptism", paras. 6, 10 with "Ministry", paras. 18, 54.
[16]*Didache*, IX; Justin Martyr, *Apology*, I, lxvi (PG 6, 427).

rites, and the second took on a meaning of its own. A theology evolved to account for the practice, and in the West admission to the Supper became an event quite separate from baptism, called 'confirmation'.[17] In some churches now, even an adult baptism is separate from confirmation and admission to communion.

None of this has been a problem for the Orthodox, for whom both rites are held together in one, baptism being immediately followed by first communion for the baptized, however young. The division of these two elements of Christian initiation in all other churches which practise paedobaptism has been achieved and maintained only at great cost, and the ambiguity it creates is probably the single greatest source of the confusion and distress in and outside the church which is the concern of these lectures. If a baptized child is excluded from the Lord's Supper, what is that child's relationship to the church? It cannot be 'membership', for 'membership' carries with it entry to the Supper. If the baptized child is not then a 'member' in that sense, how does her or his relationship to the church differ from that of an unbaptized adult adherent or enquirer?

There can be no justification of separated 'confirmation'. It establishes two stages of church membership, and so hedges the bet on infant baptism. If there is to be any rite that bestows the Spirit, not for special churchly roles but simply for Christian life as such, it must be part of baptism, for that is what baptism is supposed to do. If infants can be baptized, they must be 'confirmed' then and there or never. If infants

[17]See e.g. J. N. D. Kelly, *Early Christian Doctrine*, Adam and Charles Black, 1977, pp. 432ff.; Joseph Martos, *Doors to the Sacred*, SCM, 1981, ch. VII; Geoffrey Wainwright, *Christian Initiation*, Lutterworth, 1969, pp. 29ff.; Piet Fransen, "Confirmation", *Sacramentum Mundi*, vol. 1, pp. 405ff.; David G. Hamilton and Finlay A. J. Macdonald, *Children at the Table*, Church of Scotland Education Department, 1982, pp. 10ff.

cannot or should not receive the Spirit, they should not be baptized. If we have a rite for the Spirit and separate it from baptism, we merely thereby make either baptism or this later rite meaningless, probably both.[18]

Those of the paedobaptism churches cannot escape the charge that by stressing the importance of adult confirmation and admission to the Lord's Supper in the way we do we relegate baptism to the status of a provisional rite, admitting the baptized to what is at best a qualified membership of the Body of Christ, whose fulfilment depends on something being done later by the baptized and the church. Infant baptism then is in itself incomplete – partial deliverance, partial rebirth in Christ, promise, but not possession. We have never really accepted paedobaptism, it seems, nor submitted to its fully rigorous logic. The root of the problem lies here, in the failure on the part of the churches of the West to adopt a thoroughgoing theology of infant baptism. The shift in the centre of gravity from (infant) baptism to (adult) confirmation is at root merely an attempt to have it both ways, to 'hedge our bets' as Jenson puts it – paedobaptism modified by a later adult rite which is an effect a believers' baptism without water. That is the entry to the church and to its Supper.

Part at least of this problem lies in what a child in the church is taken to be. In our society children are commonly described in terms of what they are not and what they do not have – they are not grown up, they are unlearned, weak, immature, spiritually, mentally and physically undeveloped. Yet when Jesus speaks of children he affirms what a child already is. It is adults who are compared unfavourably to children: Jesus calls on them to become as

[18]Jenson p. 163; see also Macdonald, "Confirmation and Profession of Faith", op. cit. pp. 10ff.

children.[19] Of course the differences between child and adult are important, but part of the difference is that adults are unfortunately no longer children. They have forgotten how to be childlike; they have lost some of the special qualities of children, such as curiosity, an instinctive trust in others, idealism, candour, a freedom from pomposity. But in Christ difference and division are not the same thing. *Divisions* are transcended, so that *difference, distinctiveness*, is able to enrich the life of the Body. There is work to be done in exploring ways in which children can make their distinctive contribution to the church's life and worship. Too readily adults use children to indulge their own nostalgia for their own childhood. As well as good hymns for children, there is a need for hymns in which adults and children can join naturally together. There are, too, largely unexplored possibilities for preaching and teaching in which children and adults can interact and learn together, instead of being separated at this most dramatic part of Christian community.

The issue of the admission of children to communion has to do with the adult-child relationship in the church, and of the bearing of baptism upon it. The common argument against admitting children to communion is that children do not and could not 'understand' communion, and that without understanding and conscious faith participation in the sacrament is meaningless. Those who argue this often seek support from Paul's advice to the Corinthian church: "For anyone who eats and drinks without discerning the body eats and drinks judgement upon himself" (I Corinthians 11: 29)[20]

[19]See Hans-Ruedi Weber, *Jesus and the Children*, World Council of Churches, 1979.

[20]"Without recognising the Body" (*Jerusalem Bible*); "without a proper sense of the Body" (Moffatt); "if he does not recognise the meaning of the Lord's body" (*Good News Bible*).

'Discerning the body' – *diakrinōn to sōma* – is taken to mean 'having a conscious awareness of the seriousness of sharing in this as members of the body of Christ'. The special circumstances in the Corinthian church which prompted this rebuke from Paul, and this whole section of the letter, are well known – cliques, snobbery, a 'them and us' attitude. Some at least of the Corinthian congregation were not remembering *what the Body is,* and what it meant to think of themselves as collectively the Body of Christ. The argument that children are defective and ineligible because they are *merely baptized* is precisely the attitude which Paul denounced in the Corinthians. Those who think like this, whatever part of the Christian community they reject, are simply not understanding what the Body is, and what belonging in it means. The implications of this are serious and damaging. To intellectualise the sacraments is to reject the very gift Christ gives in sacrament – that which is freely and unconditionally held out. All that is asked in response to the invitation is to take and eat.[21]

Baptism then affirms the unity in Christ of young and old: the inclusiveness that is in Christ defies the exclusiveness of culture, society, and the world around. This is the solidarity of baptism. For children, however, the solidarity of childhood and of the peer group is also powerful and important. Imagine two eight year olds, in the same class at school and Sunday school, living in the same street, inseparable despite the occasional row. But one is baptized and the other is not; one comes to church on Sunday with the family, while the other comes alone for the family is not interested. In their church it

[21]See Horace Bushnell, *Christian Nurture,* (1888), Yale University Press, 1967, p. 162; also Geiko Muller-Fahrenholz ed. *"and do not hinder them",* Faith and Order Paper No. 109, World Council of Churches, 1982, and Hamilton and Macdonald.

is decided to have a celebration of communion open to everyone, including children – that is, *baptized* children. One of the two friends then can take part, the other is excluded. What does this teach them about the church, about communion, and about baptism? How can this distinction between one and the other be explained to them? *We know* that theologically there is a separating in baptism; we understand, in some sense, what we leave behind when we pass through the waters. But is the solidarity of childhood not theologically significant too? And what is the difference in Christ between this unbaptized eight year old, who comes and worships every Sunday without fail in what he considers 'his church', and the forty-eight year old who lives across the street from him, who (baptized certainly) comes to church only once a year for communion? Can it conceivably mean that the Table ought to be open – that it is in Christ already open – to everyone who hears and answers, in terms of their own circumstances, an invitation to take and eat? Is the question of baptism conceivably something quite separate from the question of the Lord's Supper and who is eligible to come to it? Are baptism and the Supper really locked into one another in such a way that one can only get to the Table through baptism? or does the Supper call for another, different kind of belonging than the belonging that there is in baptism?

What do solidarity and separation in baptism tell us about eligibility for baptism? What, theologically, do they say about the regulations, the church law, the conditions upon which the churches say, in one fashion or another, that a particular individual may or may not belong? Nothing is to be gained by adopting a sentimental leniency. Baptism is a momentous and far-reaching event, the herald of a life of dying and rising in Christ, and nothing we do should minimise that. But, I have argued, the child of Christian parents is not baptized because the parents are Christian. Such a child is baptized in his or her own right. Baptism is something unique and profound between that child and God, the heavenly Father. Has the church then the right to set the parents between the child and God by judging the *parents* ineligible for *their child's* baptism? What can we say to them that is better than No? The development of the use of sponsors to get round the difficulty presented by parents who are themselves unable to profess faith is clumsy and unreal and implies that the parents, whose reason for being there is their longing to have their child baptized, have no acceptable commitment of their own to offer.

Obviously a child's parents have a key role to play in nurture, but the faith that is affirmed at infant baptism is not the faith of the parents but the faith of the church catholic represented in the local congregation. It is therefore the church's belief, not primarily or even necessarily the parents' belief, that must be secure. What the parents must be willing, indeed eager, to claim is the strength and directing of the church's belief and of the grace of God, for themselves and for their child. With that must go their readiness to collaborate with the church in nurture in the years to come. Yet that willingness and eagerness can be as genuinely pledged by parents who have not themselves been able yet to profess Christian faith, as by those who have done so years earlier. The first question to parents in many baptismal liturgies is "Do you present this child to be baptized, earnestly desiring that he/she may be grafted into Christ as a member of his body the church?" To that many parents, ineligible under current regulations, could happily and unreservedly say "I do".

Given effective pastoral support and Christian nurture for such a family it is difficult to see what in practical terms would be lacking in such a commitment. Is there any reason why there should not be an appropriate 'belonging' for such parents somewhere in the fellowship of the congregation, in the church's practice and procedure? A baptized child is as powerful a link with the church for such a household as any adult profession, if the church chooses to make it so. This is not to advocate indiscriminate baptism. Rather is it the opposite – to be more discriminating than ever about baptism, and to press home the logic of grace. The church ought to beware of the danger of taking upon itself the right to renegotiate the terms on which baptism is permissible, lest this call in question the unconditionality of the Gospel, and go behind the cross and in effect qualify what Christ has done and ratified there. The young parents of a new-born child, asking of us baptism for their child, may be reminding us that we who are already of the church stand in no closer or more privileged relation to Christ than do they and their child. There may be circumstances in which it is right and wise to say No to such a request, but our refusal must, in terms of the Gospel, be at most 'not yet' and in no case 'never'. What is it that impels us to make the sacraments matters of law instead of bearers of the Gospel, instruments of authority and power over people instead of means of grace? Perhaps in the coming years our wrestling with these two issues – children at the Lord's Supper and eligibility for baptism – will lead us out from legal fastidiousness to evangelical freedom and boldness.

The importance placed by the church on the need for baptism to mark the separation between the church and the world may owe as much to culture as to theology. We belong to a culture in which much attention is paid to the ways in which individuals are distinguished from one another. 'Individuality' is prized. But in other cultures there may be important differences in the way baptism is understood. In an illuminating account of the emergent church of the Masai in Kenya the writer describes how after a lengthy period of instruction and preparation the moment for baptism arrives:

> As I was nearing the end of the evangelization of the first six Masai communities, I began looking towards baptism. So I went to the old man Ndangoya's community to prepare them for the final step.
>
> I told them I had finished the imparting of the Christian message inasmuch as I could ... Now it was up to them. They could accept or reject it ... If they did accept it there would be baptism. However baptism wasn't automatic. Over the course of the year it had taken me to instruct them, I had gotten to know them very well indeed.
>
> So I stood in front of the assembled community and began: "This old man sitting here has missed too many of our instruction meetings. He was always out herding cattle. He will not be baptized with the rest. These two on this side will be baptized because they always attended, and understood very well what we talked about. So did this young mother. She will be baptized. But that man there has obviously not understood the instructions. And that lady there has scarcely believed the gospel message. They cannot be baptized. And this warrior has not shown enough effort ..."
>
> The old man, Ndangoya, stopped me politely but firmly, "Padri, why are you trying to break us up and separate us? During this whole year that you have been teaching us, we have talked about these things when you were not here, at night around the fire. Yes, there have been lazy ones in this community. But they have been helped by those with much energy. There are stupid ones in the community, but they have been helped by those who are intelligent. Yes, there are ones with little faith in this village, but they have been helped

by those with much faith. Would you turn out and drive off the lazy ones and the ones with little faith and the stupid ones? From the first day I have spoken for these people. And I speak for them now. Now, on this day one year later, I can declare for them and for all this community, that we have reached the step in our lives where we can say, 'We believe' "[22]

The same insight appears in a story from a very different setting – from the church in China, growing dramatically in the wake of the new freedom that has come since the end of the repressive years of cultural revolution:

> Today, nineteen churches with a membership of over seven thousand have been restored or built in Xuwen County. This figure is more than double that prior to liberation.

> Surprisingly, except for the few who were baptized prior to 1950, the overwhelming majority of the present Christians in Xuwen are unbaptized . . . Although relatively untutored, the commitment of Xuwen's Christians to Christ is clear enough. The decision to follow the Lord is a family affair as much as a personal choice. In China's rural areas, to turn one's back on traditional religious practices means to sever relations with the past completely. In other words they denounce and burn the traditional gods of folk religion. If any one member of the family is not yet ready to take this step, the family as a whole will not declare itself Christian. This practice is one which keeps the value of family harmony intact. Individual family members who feel the call to follow the teachings of Jesus wait patiently and lovingly within the household until all members choose the Christian path, thus avoiding the discord, suspicion and denouncements that often marked conversions throughout China in the past. Therefore, when

[22]Vincent J. Donovan, *Christianity Rediscovered: an Epistle from the Masai*, SCM, 1978, p. 91f.

asking about the number of Christians in a given village or area, people always speak in terms of the number of Christian households first. Individual Christians are the rare exception.[23]

Some deeply rooted Western assumptions about baptism are challenged here, not merely in terms of cultural comparisons but also in terms of theological sensitivity, and powerful significance is given to the principle of baptismal solidarity.

The thrust of baptism is however not merely towards solidarity in the church, but beyond that to solidarity with the world. This is far from plain in the way it is widely understood by Christians, or portrayed in the rite itself – indeed rather the opposite. Says one writer,

> It is perhaps not without significance that in many of our baptismal liturgies the world receives no better mention than to be bracketted with the flesh and the devil from which fearsome trio we pray to be delivered.[24]

The Christian's life lies in the life of Christ, and beginning with the baptism and culminating in the death towards which the baptism pointed, Jesus gave himself wholly to the world. It was in the world, for the world, with all its ambiguities and contradictions, that the Father's will was to be done. The baptism with which he was baptized meant redemptive solidarity with sinners and failures, with the alienated, the poor, and the powerless. He points his followers to the world not as that from which to flee but as the setting in which to live, to witness, to serve, to take up the cross, and to make

[23]*Bridge – Church Life in China Today*, Tao Fong Shan Ecumenical Centre, Hong Kong, No. 22, March–April 1987, p. 4.
[24]Geoffrey Ainger, "The Local Congregation as the Dangerous Experiment of the Church", unpublished paper.

disciples, and that is where he would be with them, to the end of the age. "I do not pray that thou shouldest take them out of the world, but that thou shouldest keep them from the evil one . . . As thou didst send me into the world, so I have sent them into the world" (John 17: 15, 18). Baptism is not out of the world and into some alternative religious realm. It is into the world, there to discern and share the life of the kingdom of God. Instead of a rescue into the safety of the baptized community this is a commissioning sacrament which calls Christians out into the world to be the body of Christ there. The world from which baptism separates is the world in its self-confidence and self-sufficiency, the world that lives by what it can grasp and keep, the world that seizes for itself what rightly belongs to others, whether it be freedom or land, work or responsibility, identity or dignity – 'a world without hope and without God' (Ephesians 2: 12).

Many do not know how to bring themselves – the existential reality of their living – into the worship and witness of the church. How can we help them see that that very reality, that worldliness that is their life, is already baptized into Christ, not by what we seek to do, but by what he has already done, once for all? Many do not see how to carry the 'Christianity' that is in them and that they represent out into worldly living again. How can we help them see that 'baptized into Christ' they are baptized into his risen life in the world, and that that is the sphere of redemption, of the inbreaking of the kingdom? Baptism is what makes the connection: in it, Gospel and life, church and world, eternity and time, come together in us.

Where we 'belong' – home, neighbourhood, nation, culture, and ultimately our historical time and place – we belong, by baptism, in a new way. We are there now as women and men, girls and boys 'in Christ', and so as those in whom there is a new creation, in whom the old has passed away and the new has come (II Corinthians 5: 17). Baptism is not an acquisition but a vocation. We enter into the vocation that is Christ's, and so is ours also, to preach good news to the poor, to proclaim release to the captives, and recovery of sight to the blind, to set at liberty those who are oppressed, to proclaim the acceptable year of the Lord (Luke 4: 18–19). How precisely that is to be fulfilled in this one or that will have to be discovered, but all that we do and are as those baptized and sent will pattern itself on that vision. There is no alternative vocation.[25]

[25]See *Baptism, Eucharist and Ministry*, "Baptism", para 10.

Chapter Six

CELEBRATION

The importance of a sacrament for the Christian life lies not merely in its meaning for Christians, but also in its ability to communicate that meaning – its ability, in other words, to speak for itself. Sacrament and Word are welded to one another so fast that we cannot participate in the one without hearing the other. A sacrament is more than an illustration of a Gospel truth; it so embodies the truth in its very action that as we take part in it we find ourselves being caught up in the Gospel it proclaims. Baptism and the Lord's Supper have this quality of immediacy because Jesus chose immersion in water and the sharing of bread and wine as images of the suffering, dying and rising by which he would confront the power of sin and death, and make new life, and a new world, possible. When, like Jesus, we are baptized, when, like Jesus, we break bread and share wine, we call to mind what these actions meant to him and mean for us because of him.

So although in one sense a sacrament tells a story, it in fact does more: it draws us into the telling of the story in such a way that it becomes our story too. The New Testament word for this is *anamnesis*; it is the word Paul uses in I Corinthians 11 to describe what happens in the sacrament when Christians respond to Jesus' invitation to 'do this'. In this we do not merely remember a distant Jesus of the past. He is re-called, called back, into our time and place. What was true and real there and then becomes true and real here and now. Our story, even as we live it, becomes part of the Story which centres on him. What at first seems 'once upon a time' becomes contemporary.[1] This belongs to what is

[1]See e.g. A. G. Hebert, "Memory, Memorial, Remember, Remem-

given to his disciples when they bring their lives, fears, and failures, their hunger and thirst, to the table of the Lord. It belongs to the nature of the Supper that this *anamnesis*, this fusion of present and past, happens because people *deliberately go* in their hunger and their expectation to the table. By contrast it belongs to the nature of *baptism* that people *do not need to go deliberately*, nor even consciously, through the waters to be drawn into the mystery and miracle of deliverance in Christ. Baptism is the sacrament of our helplessness, and is characteristically baptism of infants. What is recalled, God's love in Christ, is not true for us because we understand it: we only come to understand it (and indeed to go on to celebrate it in the Supper) because it happened for us.

From then on, of course, baptism goes on ministering to us. My baptism was not an isolated event, but was and is part of the ongoing, unceasing baptizing in the church, and is represented to me in every new baptism I witness and participate in. Repeatedly we recall and rediscover the momentous event that has taken place, and what it has to do with us. Although our own baptism in itself is unrepeatable, it reverberates within us, it is restated, each time we share in someone else's baptism. We may not remember our own baptism, but the astonishing realisation of what it is to have been baptized – to be a baptized person – grows and grows as the years pass. Indeed the mystery of our baptism, buried deep in our subconscious being as the mystery of our salvation

brance", in *A Theological Word Book of the Bible*, ed. Alan Richardson, SCM, 1950: "The sacrifice offered once for all and unrepeatable would be continually renewed, and become newly present".

In the family Passover celebration, the questions of the younger ones are answered by the retelling of the story, not in the third person but the first: "We were slaves to Pharaoh in Egypt, and the Lord freed us from Egypt with a mighty hand. Had not the Holy One, praised be He, delivered our people from Egypt, then we, our children, and our children's children would still be enslaved". See Exodus 13:3, Deuteronomy 6: 20–25.

is buried deep in our human history, is itself an important part of that history. God's love in Christ for us goes back beyond memory and consciousness.

Obviously this has implications for the liturgy of baptism. The liturgy which encases the sacrament must faithfully and unambiguously express what the sacrament itself tells. Is this possible? F. W. Dillistone has doubts that it can:

> There is need today for a thorough re-examination by Reformed theologians of the *form* of the baptismal rite and for a resolute facing of the question whether a passing through the waters is any longer an appropriate symbol of the initial establishment of the Covenant. There is little likelihood that a widespread adoption of the practice of baptism by immersion will take place within the majority of the Churches of the Reformed tradition. The question is whether any other form of initiatory rite can more adequately symbolise the great truths of the covenant grace of God and justification by faith.[2]

However even a tankful of water is still only symbolic, for what is symbolised is so terrifyingly, so overwhelmingly destructive, that no symbolic action or element can do more than hint at it. Total immersion is no more than what a thousand people do every day in the local swimming pool for fun. On the other hand a damp-handed dab is so minimal, so completely off the scale at the other end, that it is not even symbolic. Water poured, washed over the head, is recognisable and matter of fact, in infant baptism visible to those close by, in adult baptism palpable to the candidate – water unmistakeably there, and wet.

What about the words? Major changes in the baptism liturgy have been made by many churches in the past twenty

---

[2] *Christianity and Symbolism*, p. 219. But see Barth, op.cit. p. 61.

years. The Roman Catholic post-Vatican II rite is direct and simple, restores to parents their proper role in the baptism of their children and beyond it, and regards godparents not as supplanting but as supporting the parents, willing to take a special interest in the child's upbringing and nurture. Although other symbolism is used (the white robe, and the lighted candle for instance), in prayers and readings the full imagery of water is clearly presented. Similar work, though less bold and thoroughgoing has been done on the Anglican rite for *The Alternative Service Book*[3] though proxy vows by godparents still linger on. The Order for Holy Baptism in the *Church of Scotland Book of Common Order 1979*[4] is disappointing, with little sign of fresh thinking, and with no reference at all to 'dying and rising in Christ' and to the deliverance understanding of baptism which I have argued must be at the heart of an adequate and scripturally faithful rite. This emphasis has however been imaginatively achieved in the new Rite for the Baptism of a Child of the Reformed Church of France. Here the imagery of 'going through the waters' is clear and explicit. Baptism as washing, as drowning and deliverance, and as birth, is spoken of simply but biblically, and no one taking part could fail to recognise what baptism means to the church. The French rite contains something more – a direct address to the child, immediately before baptizing:

> Little child, for you Jesus Christ has come, has struggled and suffered; for you he has gone through the agony of Gethsemane and the darkness of Calvary; for you he cried

[3] Hodder & Stoughton, 1980, pp. 214ff. See also notes on "Family Baptism", p. 225f: "When children who are not old enough to answer for themselves are to be baptized at the same time as their parents, the parents answer the questions for themselves and for their children".

[4] The Saint Andrew Press, 1979, pp. 46ff.

out 'It is accomplished'. For you he triumphed over death . . . Yes for you, little child, though you know nothing yet of this. But thus is the word of the apostle confirmed, 'We love God, because he loved us first'.

Without any trace of sentimentality these words succeed in acknowledging that the child is being baptized *as a child*. The child is not merely *spoken about* but is *spoken to*, yet in terms which are appropriate and evangelical. The point of this is that the child 'knows nothing yet of this', and so the pattern and the logic of grace is vividly set forth. At last we have the makings of a satisfactory liturgy of infant baptism.

The Church of Scotland's Panel on Worship has published a new Order for Baptism, drawing upon the French Order in some respects. [5] Regrettably, the 'instruction' of the French Order is replaced here by the introduction from *The Book of Common Order 1979*, very slightly expanded but still lacking any reference to the overwhelming, destroying image of water, and even to the dying and rising significance of baptism. A helpful new feature however is that the questions to parents concerning their responsiblities towards their child, and the affirmation of faith by congregation and parents together using the Apostles' Creed, are placed after the baptism:

It had been felt that this question (regarding Christian nurture for the child), occurring as it did immediately before the baptism, gave an appearance of conditionality which was inappropriate to the sacrament which spoke so eloquently of grace. The question now finds a happier place after the baptism and together with the congregation's commitment.[6]

[5] The Panel on Worship of the Church of Scotland, Oxford University Press, 1986.

[6] Foreword, p. 1.

118

R. W. Jenson writes of the liturgy of baptism,

> More than any other sacrament, baptism has recently been
> buried beneath quantities of extremely disembodied
> explanation and exhortation, and tenuously relevant prayer.
> This is partly in sheer compensation for vanished actions, lest
> the whole performance shrink to an experiential point. It is
> partly a futile last-minute attempt to make up for missed
> preparation and testing of the neophytes or parents. And
> above all, it is an entirely futile attempt verbally to impose
> meaning on a visible word too attenuated to speak for itself.
> At least for the foreseeable future, the motto of baptismal
> orders must be: less talking, more doing.[7]

The wordiness about which Jenson complains is especially
cumbersome in the introduction to the rite. In the first place,
the practice of reciting the Commission of Matthew 28: 18–
20, as if it were the dominical institution of baptism, must
be questioned. To describe it as 'the command of the risen
Christ'[8] makes assumptions about which most New Testament
scholars would have serious doubts. In any case, it is not
a command about baptizing but about 'making disciples'.
Discipling involves teaching and baptizing. It is plain from
the context that these go together and that the community
already understands this. Neither teaching nor baptism is
explained, and so to quote this as instruction about baptism
at the beginning of the rite is pointless, if not indeed
misleading. Nothing would be lost, and much would be
gained, if the Commission were left out altogether. What
instead would be much more helpful and edifying would be
quotation or paraphrase of Romans 6, coupled with verses
from such Psalms as 93 or 95, or Isaiah 43: 1– 2 or 54: 9–10.

[7] op. cit. p. 173.
[8] *The Alternative Service Book 1980*, p. 244; *A Book of Services*, p. 44; *The Book of Common Order 1979*, p. 46; *An Order for Holy Baptism*, p. 2.

As well as 'instruction', and distinct from it, there must in baptism be a clear remembering, *anamnesis*, of Jesus. If this is central to the Supper, then it is every bit as central here, for it tells of The Baptism, the salvation story which the sacrament celebrates and into which it summons and leads each newcomer. As we have seen, the French Order places recital or recalling of the saving work of Christ in the address to the child immediately before the act of baptizing. It could find a place also in the pre-baptismal prayer, which tends to be reduced to little more than an abrupt and somewhat mysterious blessing of the water, but it is out of place, I think in the introduction. We must resist the temptation to stuff as much doctrine as we can into the introduction – as if in the hope that something at least will stick in the minds of the hearers. The introduction is the place for simple, direct reminder of scriptural images. Without them how can we expect to understand the mystery and the drama that follows?

Let us also be scrupulous in avoiding stereotypes. Babies are always, it is implied, strong, healthy, free from physical or mental handicap; parents, without exception, have planned and wanted this child, and are at one in their love for each other and for their child; families always have two parents, neither of whom were previously married to anyone else and are unencumbered with children from another marriage. Typecasting like this robs the sacrament of reality and credibility. What is said must be altogether true and appropriate for the family group at the centre of the occasion, and also for adults and children who are present in the congregation. The mention of 'parents' will need amending in the case of a one-parent family; references to 'little ones' will sound absurd when the one being baptized is a sturdy five year old; and nothing that is said should fail to be true for a Down's syndrome babe whose parents are only beginning to come to terms with the difficulties which lie ahead for them and their child. In this sacrament which testifies to the all-inclusive love of God anything exclusive, said or implied, can have no place.

Such care over the details is important not only for infant baptism: the liturgy of baptism of adults in paedobaptist churches also needs to be overhauled. If infant baptism is truly the norm, and so the best and plainest expression of our theology of baptism, centering on the priority of grace, then the adult rite must conform to the infant rite. If it does not, we end up with two distinct and contradictory theologies of baptism. If Baptist churches unambiguously express in their rite the theology behind believers' baptism as they see it, then non-Baptist churches must be equally rigorous and unambiguous in what both the infant and the adult rite express. Baptism for an adult must be as unconditional as it is for a child. The adult comes to this as a little child. There can be only one baptism, not two.

In practice most adults seeking baptism will have already undergone teaching and preparation in faith and life, but the liturgy ought not to suggest that he or she is being baptized following and because of profession of faith, repentance, and dedication of life. Liturgically as well as theologically that should follow the baptizing, which should be allowed to speak clearly of the grace of God meeting the openness and readiness of the one being baptized. "Thus is the word of the apostle fulfilled: 'We love God because he first loved us'". *Then*, of course, the newly baptized can join with the congregation in declaring the faith of the church; *then* come the promises and the self-dedication. There is no reason at all why the church should not devise a rite which is both meaningful for the adult yet faithful to the logic of baptism. Adult baptism based on an infant baptism norm is fundamentally different from believer's baptism based upon repentance and faith, and the liturgy ought to make the difference quite clear.[9]

Help is needed, not only pastorally as we have seen but also liturgically, for those who badly want to get in touch again with their infant baptism, and to recover and release its power and its grace for their adult living. A rite and an occasion are needed for the renewal and recollection of baptism that is as clear, imaginative and theologically apt as the sacrament itself. The Methodist Covenant Service, used particularly on the first Sunday of a new year, is a well-established example. More recently, other churches have devised and introduced similar services.[10] It is often said that the eucharist is the natural and obvious act of renewing one's baptism. It is more likely that nothing short of a distinct rite specifically for this purpose, repeated regularly year by year, will satisfy a real and understandable appeal from many (and some of the most committed) in the church.

It looks at first sight as if such a rite should centre on a reaffirming of promises and an act of rededication. But is this really what is needed? More likely the need is to reach back to the baptism in infancy, when grace surrounded and bore us, long before we knew or understood, or could begin to respond. It is the immediacy and generosity of that grace that is the miracle of our living, not just back there in the past but here and now in the present, and to the end of our days, and beyond. Without that continuing grace, always first, always a gift given before asked for, faith cannot be found and declared, sins cannot be recognised and confessed, forgiveness cannot be understood and accepted, and

[9] See Appendix, pp. 126ff.

[10] e.g. Joint Liturgical Group, *Holy Week Services*, SPCK, 1983, pp. 36ff and 87f and *The Alternative Service Book 1980*, pp. 275 ff. See too Wainwright, *Doxology*, p. 322f.

commitment cannot be offered and lived. Again and again we need opportunities for readiness and expectancy in which everything in us is still and open. So much of living, even of Christian living, is giving, doing, striving: we need occasions to learn again how to stop, and receive as little children.

Earlier I referred to something F. W. Dillistone has written:

> To find a way of allowing baptism to exercise its power within the Christian community at the deepest level of the human psyche is one of the most urgent tasks of our day.[11]

The paradox is that what is received as little children is for our living as adults. The liturgy of the gathered community of the baptized has to be matched by a spirituality for the community when scattered in the world. Only when that spirituality, that Christian worldly living, has become conscious and understood can we say that baptism has fully done its work. The celebration of baptism begins in the sanctuary, but finishes far beyond it. Worldy living is very much a matter of struggle and search and finding, of being reborn again and again, of dying and rising. It will be so in the inwardness of personal moments of letting go and of moving on, often most starkly in the experiences of grief and loss. It will be so also in the life we live with others in the community, local or global: the surges and the storms may at times be economic or political. There can be no better key to the understanding of all this, and to the living of it, than the great themes of baptism. Baptism is more than a motif: it is the foundation of a spirituality, it is how Christians are to understand what is happening to them. And it is this for Christians because it was this for Christ.

[11] op. cit. p. 187.

★　　　★　　　★

We have now explored three images for baptism –
washing, dying and rising, and birth. They are not each of
equal weight: are we however to choose the one we like
best? Christians have a compulsive urge towards theological
tidiness – everything neat and in its place, no rough edges, no
loose ends. But the life which we are called as Christians to
live cannot be so tidy, cannot have everything in its predicted
place, cannot stand still. So we need a cluster of images to
make sense of it, and of the grace and power and meaning
God gives to it. The passage from day to day, from Sunday
to Sunday, from each Easter to the next, will be marked by
many critical moments. Some of these moments will feel
gentle and reassuring, as if we were being cleansed and healed.
Some will feel terrifying, as if we were being overwhelmed
by forces far beyond our control, and it will be as if,
exhausted and done, we are amazingly delivered and brought
back to life. And some will feel like an astonishing liberation,
when all will seem new, as if seen and known for the first
time, and it will be as if we are born anew. These are living
moments, and we shall be poor if we do not know them all,
again and again.

Yet these experiences will only yield their meaning and
their power if the people to whom they happen are already
learning what to watch out for. Because baptism points both
inwards to the inner space we inhabit, with its mysterious
pulses and rhythms, and also outwards to the world we share
with others, where grace is lived by, it concerns *what we
know*, what we are familiar with. Baptism is not primarily or
in any important sense a doctrine: it is how Christians
understand life, because it is how Jesus has taught us to
understand life. It is to do with where we come from, and
where ultimately we are going – but it is above all to do
with where we are now. We should be encouraged to make

our baptism our own. We are not to be intimidated by it, or anxious in case we say something wrong or silly about it. Our deepest longings and discoveries, our little rebirths, our dyings and risings, are not trivial. They are real, they are the baptism we are baptized with. They are how it is between God and us. We are speaking not of religion so much as of life in the world. In the end of the day it is there that baptism is celebrated. And there it bears witness in us to what has already happened in Jesus Christ, and what is still to come through Jesus Christ. It is the sacrament of living between the 'already' and the 'not yet'. If nothing is already true for us, already done and decided for us, life is intolerable, for it has no secure foundation. And if there is no certainty that eventually wrongs will be put right – my wrongs among them – that what is distorted will be mended, and what is broken healed, then life now is intolerable, for it has no future. Baptism anchors us to what is already true, said and done in Christ – and therefore incapable of being denied, unsaid, undone. And baptism at the same time holds us to hope, that what is not yet, for everyone and for each, will at length be finished. Our baptism tells us that we do not have to go to Calvary, for Christ has already set Calvary in the past. When we suffer, it is not in futility and despair; suffering will not overwhelm us, and death will not destroy us. Baptism is the sacramental sign of our living, celebrating in us that what is happening to us, and what may yet happen to us in the future, has become part of the saving, recreating work of God.[12]

In our forsakenness we will still know we belong; in darkness we will rejoice; and in dying we will live. For it is into such a life as this, in Christ, that we are baptized.

[12] See Barth, op. cit. p. 63f.

Appendix

AN ORDER FOR BAPTISM

The minister addresses the people:

In the Sacrament of Baptism we celebrate what God in Christ Jesus has done for us, and we enter upon the new life which God by the Spirit opens to us. Jesus went down to death, but out of the dark depths of sorrow and suffering he rose to life and victory. This was his Baptism. This we recall each time someone is baptized. Baptism means 'coming through the waters', to life and salvation in Jesus Christ.

The Scriptures say:

The Lord who created you says, 'Do not be afraid – I will save you.
   I have called you by name – you are mine.
When you pass through deep waters, I will be with you:
your troubles will not overwhelm you'. (Isaiah 43: 1–2)

Surely you know (writes St. Paul) that when we were baptized into union with Christ Jesus, we were baptized into union with his death. By our baptism, then, we were buried with him and shared his death, in order that, just as Christ was raised from death by the glorious power of the Father, so also we might live a new life. (Romans 6: 3–4)[1]
This is the promise of God: this we celebrate and claim again now.

[1] *Good News Bible: Today's English Version.* Or Psalm 93: 1, 4; 95: 1–5; Colossians 1: 12–13; 2: 12; Titus 3: 4–7.

Let us pray:

We praise you, Lord God of Creation, for out of chaos and darkness you brought order and life;

we praise you, Lord Jesus Christ of Calvary, for through the baptism of suffering and struggle you have brought deliverance and hope;

we praise you, Holy Spirit of Pentecost, for by your power and indwelling you bring new birth and new life for us all.

In remembrance of what you have done, and in joyful trust, we bring this child (*or* N———)[2] to the waters of baptism now.

Let your Word speak, your Spirit descend,
that our faith become trust in your promises,
this common water become the very waters of baptism,
and this child of yours become the newest member of your holy people;
through Jesus Christ our Lord.

or

In what we now do, and in the means we use, do your great work.
By the waters of baptism make *her* one with yourself and one with us;
through Jesus Christ our Lord.

---

[2]The one being baptized can be addressed as 'child', 'sister', 'brother', or by name, as seems most natural. Likewise of course 'she' or 'her' becomes 'he' or 'him' as appropriate.

The minister addresses the one to be baptized:

(*at the baptism of a child*)

Little child . . .
for you Jesus Christ has come, has struggled and suffered;
for you he has gone through the agony of Gethsemane and
the darkness of Calvary;
for you he cried out 'It is accomplished';
for you he triumphed over death . . .
Yes, for you, little child, though you know nothing yet of
this.
But thus is the word of the apostle confirmed,
'We love God, because he first loved us'.[3]

(*at the baptism of an adult*)

N——
for you, Jesus Christ has come, has struggled and suffered;
for you he has gone through the agony of Gethsemane and
the darkness of Calvary;
for you he cried out 'It is accomplished';
for you he triumphed over death . . .
Yes, for you he did all this, before ever you knew of it.
But thus is the word of the apostle confirmed,
'We love God, because he first loved us'.[4]

N—— I baptize you, in the name of the Father, and of the
Son, and of the Holy Spirit.
The blessing of God Almighty, Father, Son and Holy Spirit,
descend upon you and dwell in your heart for ever.

[3]Liturgy of Baptism, Eglise Reformée de France.
[4]The Address to the Child adapts readily for the baptism of an adult.

*(Here the act of reception into membership or admission to the
Lord's Supper may be included*

The minister lays hands upon the newly baptized, saying:

Confirm, O Lord, this your servant,
    that *she* may continue yours for ever,
    and daily increase in your Holy Spirit,
    until *she* comes to your everlasting kingdom

or

The God of all grace,
    who has called you by Christ Jesus,
    confirm you by his Holy Spirit.)

At the baptism of a child, the minister now addresses the parents:

Your child now belongs with us to God in Christ. From this
day the Christian community is *her* home, and there will
always be a place within it kept for *her*. You are witnesses of
her baptism. Tell *her* of it; unfold for *her* the treasure *she* has
been given this day; so that *she* may understand *her* baptism
and, as *she* grows, make *her* own response in faith and love.[5]

Do you then promise, God being your helper, to make your
home a Christian home, and to bring your child up in the
faith of Christ and in the fellowship of his church?

Answer: I do.

[5] *An Order for Holy Baptism*, Church of Scotland Panel on Worship,
Oxford University Press, 1986, p. 4.

At the baptism of an adult, the minister addresses the newly-baptized:

You now belong with us to God in Christ. From this day the Christian community is your home, and there will always be a place within it kept for you.

Do you then promise, as a member of Christ's church, to confess him before others, to serve him in your daily work, and to walk in his ways all the days of your life?

Answer: I do.

The minister addresses the congregation:

Sisters and brothers, this day N—— has been baptized in your midst. Do you, the Christian community in this place, promise to welcome and uphold *her*, to nurture and strengthen *her*, in the fellowship of the Spirit and the bond of peace?

Answer· We do.

The congregation may say or sing:

The Lord bless you and keep you; the Lord make his face to shine upon you and be gracious unto you. The Lord lift up his countenance upon you, and give you peace.

The minister continues:

Once again in this sacrament the sign of our salvation has been set before us. Once again in this sacrament our baptism has been brought back to us. Let us reaffirm together the faith of the church:

I believe . . .

Here may follow an Act of Recollection of Baptism, the congregation saying together:

Christ be with me, Christ within me,
Christ behind me, Christ before me,
Christ beside me, Christ to win me,
Christ to comfort and restore me,
Christ beneath me, Christ above me,
Christ in quiet, Christ in danger,
Christ in hearts of all that love me,
Christ in mouth of friend and stranger.

or

God be in my head, and in my understanding;
God be in mine eyes, and in my looking;
God be in my mouth, and in my speaking;
God be in my heart, and in my thinking;
God be at mine end, and at my departing.

Prayers

God of grace and love,
once again we have heard your Word and witnessed your sign;

once again we, long since baptized, have remembered our
beginning and our growing,
as sons and daughters of the Father;
once again we are made new, by your Spirit.

Now lead this child of yours, your chosen one, out into life.
May *she* have love to hold *her*,
trust to guide *her*,
and joy to delight *her*.
May *she* find a world that will welcome *her*,
and a Saviour beside *her*, always and everywhere.

(Guide *her* parents, in their care for *her*.
Give to this family the blessings of courage and wisdom,
laughter and peace,
and the love that will endure all things.)

Touch us all again this day
with the remembrance of our baptism.
Give us new lives for old,
new spirits, new faith, new commitment,
in place of all that has grown tired, and stale, and dead in our
lives.
So may we rise and go from here,
to whatever awaits us,
in joy and trust.

O God,
in whose church there is but one Lord, one Faith, one Baptism,
grant us ever to acknowledge that Jesus Christ is Lord,
to profess with our whole lives the one true faith,
and ever to live in love and unity with all who are baptized
in his name,
through Jesus Christ our Lord.

Eternal God,
as we rejoice in each other's company here,
we rejoice also to remember those who have already passed
on their way,
through the very waters of death into life eternal,
the communion of all the saints.
These we would follow,
faithfully and expectantly,
in the strength of our baptism in Christ Jesus our Lord,
who lives and reigns, and is worshipped and glorified,
with you, Father, and the Holy Spirit,
one God for ever.

INDEX